AN ETHIC
FOR CHRISTIANS
AND OTHER ALIENS
IN A STRANGE LAND

by the same author

A SECOND BIRTHDAY: a personal
confrontation with illness, pain, and death

MY PEOPLE IS THE ENEMY: an
autobiographical polemic

COUNT IT ALL JOY: reflections
on faith, doubt, and temptation

DISSENTER IN A GREAT SOCIETY: a Christian
view of America in crisis

FREE IN OBEDIENCE: the radical Christian life

A PRIVATE AND PUBLIC FAITH

as coauthor with Anthony Towne

SUSPECT TENDERNESS: the ethics
of the Berrigan witness

THE BISHOP PIKE AFFAIR

AN ETHIC
FOR CHRISTIANS
AND OTHER ALIENS
IN A STRANGE LAND

William Stringfellow

**WORD BOOKS,
PUBLISHER**
Waco, Texas

for

Thomas Merton

contents

AN ETHIC
FOR CHRISTIANS
AND OTHER ALIENS
IN A STRANGE LAND

By the waters of Babylon,
  there we sat down and wept,
when we remembered Zion.
On the willows there
  we hung up our lyres.
For there our captors
  required of us songs,
and our tormentors, mirth, saying,
  "Sing us one of the songs of Zion!"

How shall we sing the Lord's song
  in a strange land?
If I forget you, O Jerusalem,
  let my right hand wither!
Let my tongue cleave to the roof of my mouth,
  if I do not remember you,
if I do not set Jerusalem
  above my highest joy!

Remember, O Lord, against the Edomites
  the day of Jerusalem,
how they said, "Rase it, rase it!
  Down to its foundations!"
O daughter of Babylon, you devastator!
  Happy shall he be who requites you
  with what you have done to us!
Happy shall he be who takes your little ones
  and dashes them against the rock!

Psalm 137

preface

on the
peculiarity of this book
as a tract
for these times
in America

My concern is to understand America biblically. This book—which is, simultaneously, a theological statement and a political argument —implements that concern.

The effort is to comprehend the nation, to grasp what is happening right now to the nation and to consider the destiny of the nation within the scope and style of the ethics and the ethical metaphors distinctive to the biblical witness in history.

The task is to treat the nation within the tradition of biblical politics—to understand America biblically—*not* the other way around, *not* (to put it in an appropriately awkward way) to construe the Bible Americanly. There has been much too much of the latter in this country's public life and religious ethos. There still is. I expect such indulgences to multiply, to reach larger absurdities, to become more scandalous, to increase blasphemously as America's crisis as a nation distends. To interpret the Bible for the convenience of America, as apropos as that may seem to be to any Americans, represents a radical violence to both the

14   An Ethic
                    for Christians and Other Aliens
                           in a Strange Land

character and content of the biblical message. It fosters a
fatal vanity that America is a divinely favored nation and
makes of it the credo of a civic religion which is directly
threatened by, and, hence, which is anxious and hostile
toward the biblical Word. It arrogantly misappropriates
political images from the Bible and applies them to America,
so that America is conceived of as Zion: as *the* righteous
nation, as a people of superior political morality, as a country and society chosen and especially esteemed by God. In
archetypical form in this century, material abundance, redundant productivity, technological facility, and military
predominance are publicly cited to verify the alleged divine
preference and prove the supposed national virtue. It is just
this kind of Sadducean sophistry, distorting the biblical
truth for American purposes, which, in truth, occasions the
moral turmoil which the nation so manifestly suffers today
and which, I believe, renders us a people as unhappy as we
are hopeless. It is profane, as well as grandiose, to manipu-
late the Bible in order to apologize for America. To read this
tract lucently requires (and, I trust, evokes) freedom from
temptations to violate the Bible to justify America as a
nation.

biblical politics

This book is necessarily at once theological and political
for the good reason that the theology of the Bible concerns
politics in its most rudimentary meaning and in its most
auspicious connotations.

The biblical topic *is* politics. The Bible is about the politics
of fallen creation and the politics of redemption; the politics
of the nations, institutions, ideologies, and causes of this
world and the politics of the Kingdom of God; the politics
of Babylon and the politics of Jerusalem; the politics of the
Antichrist and the politics of Jesus Christ; the politics of
the demonic powers and principalities and the politics of the
timely judgment of God as sovereign; the politics of death

biblical politics

and the politics of life; apocalyptic politics and eschatological politics.

Throughout the diversity of the biblical saga as history and as literature, the priority of politics remains prominent. The Bible expounds with extraordinary versatility, now one way and then another, and another, the singular issue of salvation—which is to say, the preemptive *political* issue. It bespeaks the reality of human life consummated in society within time in this world, now and here, as the promise of renewal and fulfillment vouchsafed for all humans and for every nation—for the whole of Creation—throughout time.

Despite the habitual malpractice of translating biblical politics as the American story, there is also the odd and contradictory custom among many Americans to denounce the truth that the Bible is political. Frequently, if incongruously, these two convictions are held concurrently by the same person, or by the same sect or church or social faction. American experience as a nation—as well as biblical scholarship—discredits any attempted Americanization of biblical politics and confounds the notion that the Bible is apolitical. What is surprising is that the latter belief persists even though so many of the biblical symbols are explicitly political—*dominion, emancipation, authority, judgment, kingdom, reconciliation* among them—and even though the most familiar biblical events are notoriously political—including the drama of Israel the holy nation, the Kingdom parables in Christ's teaching, the condemnation of Christ as King of the Jews by the imperial authorities, the persecutions of the Apostolic congregations, the controversies between Christians and zealots, the propagation of the Book of Revelation.

Well, I do not amplify the matter here, apart from noticing that the view that the Bible is politically neuter or innocuous—coupled, as it may be, ironically, with an American misuse of biblical politics—maintains wide currency in this nation. And this view sorely inhibits a biblical comprehension of America as a nation.

16

An Ethic
for Christians and Other Aliens
in a Strange Land

the authority of Revelation

In my own concern to understand America biblically, I have turned to the Book of Revelation. I realize that Revelation is not a part of the Bible to which Americans are accustomed, but I am also aware of how often and of how urgently Christians have been nurtured, edified, and inspired through it as, in diverse times and places, they have besought a credible witness in humanly oppressive circumstances. Such was the situation when the book was uttered in the first century. And so it has been subsequently, through the centuries, including within memory the extraordinary appeals to Revelation during the Nazi reign.

The quest for viable Christian style in the enveloping technological totalitarianism in America today similarly provokes attention to Revelation. The Book of Revelation is both an exciting exposition of biblical ethics and a preeminent example of the practice of biblical politics. By virtue of that fact, in the midst of the traumas of existence for persons and for institutions in contemporary America, there is much to learn from Revelation.

In this tract, I do not treat Revelation as an exegetical problem, as fascinating a subject as that is. Though I have sought to be exegetically responsible, this book does not purport to be a technical treatise; it is a polemic. Thus, mindful of the origins and uses of the text as a theological confession which at the same time is a political document, I rely upon Revelation as inspiration. In America, now, human beings need to live biblically. This *Ethic for Christians and Other Aliens in a Strange Land* is an exhortation for biblical living for which the Book of Revelation furnishes precedent in substance and style, in ethics and political tactics.

the principalities and powers

In the Babylon passages in Revelation, which this book particularly invokes, emphasis is focused on the nation as a principality and, indeed, as the archetypal principality. The principalities and powers have received little attention in American Christendom. In that context the customary propositions of moral theology concern individual decision and action and the supposed efficacy of the conviction of the individual for social renewal and societal change. To speak in a general way, in what has come to be called "the social gospel," as well as in evangelical pietism—though these have commonly represented antagonistic sides of the political and social spectrum and though each symbolizes and embraces many particular versions and factions—the view prevails that society is transformed by means of the persuasion or conversion of individuals and by the accumulative impact or geometric progression of the commitment and involvement of individuals. This is really a social ethic of osmosis. It has been dominant throughout the American churches, despite the widely divergent opinions concerning specific political issues or social policies among so-called activists on one hand, or among assorted pietists on the other.

As a social ethic, this concentration upon the efficacious potential of individuals, even when computed geometrically, suffers the distortion of any partial truth. That is, what it overlooks or omits is more significant than that which it asserts and affirms. What is most crucial about this situation, biblically speaking, is the failure of moral theology, in the American context, to confront the principalities—the institutions, systems, ideologies, and other political and social powers—as militant, aggressive, and immensely influential creatures in this world as it is. Any ethic of social renewal, any effort in social regeneration—regardless of what it concretely projects for human life in society—is certain to be perpetually frustrated unless account is taken of these realities named principalities and their identities and how they operate vis-à-vis one another and in relation to human beings.

The neglect in moral theology, as that has developed within the American ethos, of the demonic powers is star-

18

**An Ethic
for Christians and Other Aliens
in a Strange Land**

tling and virtually inexplicable, when one pauses to think of the exceptional proliferation and sophistication of institutional life, as well as that of other species of the principalities, in technological culture. This void in theology and ethics is even more astounding when one notices evidence of the political dominance of the principalities in documentation like *The Pentagon Papers. The Greening of America,* for another instance, is descriptive of the principalities in action, though this is substantially vitiated by the author's overwhelming sentimentality concerning human capabilities, intimating that the author does not realize the demonic character of the very powers he describes. Eisenhower's famous farewell address as President, with its admonition about the insatiability of the military-industrial complex, or Ralph Nader's diligent exposés of corporate assaults and importunities against human life are additional public signs of the familiarity and vitality of the principalities and powers in American society, even though few may recognize kinship of the principalities with the moral reality of death. Need Watergate be mentioned?

Americans—including professed Christians, who have biblical grounds to be wiser—remain, it seems, astonishingly obtuse about these powers. They seldom impute to them personality or integrity as creatures, and commonly deem institutions and similar principalities as subject to human sponsorship, patronage, and control. Yet to be ignorant or gullible or ingenuous about the demons, to underestimate the inherent capacities of the principalities, to fail to notice the autonomy of these powers as creatures abets their usurpation of human life and their domination of human beings.

Part of the message of the Book of Revelation which is, I believe, empirically verified in the present day as much as in the day Revelation was uttered, is that any social concern of human beings which neglects or refuses to deal with the principalities with due regard for their own dignity is delusive, while any social change predicated upon mere human action—whether prompted by a so-called social gospel or motivated by some pietism—is doomed.

the principalities and powers

In short, to behold America biblically requires comprehension of the powers and principalities as they appear and as they abound in this world, even, alas, in America. The Book of Revelation is pertinent for Americans because it so urgently elucidates the power of death incarnate in the principalities, notably in the nation.

a naïveté about the Fall

Contending as I do that Americans are, in a rudimentary way, biblically illiterate and that the radical moral confusion within the nation stems from that illiteracy, it is possible to state my concern in different words, and blatantly: *most Americans are grossly naïve or remarkably misinformed about the Fall.* Even within the American churchly environment, there prevails too mean, too trivial, too narrow, too gullible a view of the biblical doctrine and description of the Fall. Especially within the churches there is a discounting of how the reality of fallenness (not the reality of evil, but the reality of fallenness: of loss of identity and of alienation, of basic disorientation and of death) afflicts the whole of Creation, not human beings alone but also the principalities, the nations included. This book treats the meaning of the Fall as the era in which persons and nations and other creatures exist in profound and poignant and perpetual strife and, thus, as the realm in which ethics are constantly at issue. This book is about the political significance of the Fall.

The Fall is where the nation is. The Fall is the locus of America. Apprehending that much is decisive, it seems to me, as to any possibilities of transcending the malaise which Americans lately suffer, in multifarious ways, concerning the nation's destiny. Since the climax of America's glorification as a nation—in the ostensible American victory in World War II, most lucidly and aptly symbolized in Hiroshima—Americans have become so beleaguered by anxiety and fatigue, so bemused and intimidated, so beset by a sense of impotence and by intuitions of calamity, that they have,

20

**An Ethic
for Christians and Other Aliens
in a Strange Land**

for the most part, become consigned to despair. The people have been existing under a state of such interminable warfare that it seems normative. There is little resistance to the official Orwellian designation of war as peace, nor does that rhetorical deception come near exhausting the ways in which the people have found the government to be unworthy of credence or trust. Racial conflict has been suppressed by an elaborate apartheid; products which supposedly mean abundance or convenience turn out to contaminate or jeopardize life; the environment itself is rendered hostile; there is pervasive babel; privacy is a memory because surveillance is ubiquitous; institutional coercion of human beings has proliferated relentlessly. Whatever must be said of earlier times, in the past quarter century America has become a technological totalitarianism in which hope, in its ordinary human connotations, is being annihilated.

Oh, there has been spasmodic relief. Martin Luther King had a dream. There have been some glimpses of Camelot and, perchance, even of Jerusalem. Many have thought, briefly, that hope for the nation could be restored if only good men would succeed the wicked in high places, particularly in the White House. I suppose that protest and dissent and rebellion can all be interpreted as signs of hope as readily as they can be accounted expressions of despair. Still, at least since Hiroshima, Americans have been learning, harshly, redundantly, that they inherit or otherwise possess no virtue or no vanity which dispels the condition of death manifest everywhere in the nation.

It is exactly because of this vehemence in the American situation as a nation that little space is spent in this book upon social analysis or social criticism, save where, occasionally, such has seemed illustratively pertinent. For the most part, however, this effort does not expand the contemporary literature of social critique, though it presupposes a reader's acquaintance with that literature, possibly including some of my own contributions to it. Probing and diagnosing the nation has been overdone or, at the least, done

a naïveté about the Fall

enough for the time being. There is simply a point at which social analysis must be validated in action or else it becomes morbid, self-indulgent, and misleading, compounding the very issues it professes to clarify. There comes a moment when words must either become incarnated or the words, even if literally true, are rendered false.

So this tract seeks to move beyond analysis to ethics, and from ethics to politics. It identifies the apparent chaos, the deadly atmosphere which pervades America now as the essential truth of existence for nations and other principalities in estrangement and conflict with human beings—a condition which the Bible designates as the Fall. It appeals to the authority and style of the Book of Revelation because Revelation contains a parable of the fallenness of the nations and similar powers, and because Revelation offers a witness to the biblical politics which cope with that condition.

How can human beings live in hope in the presence of the moral reality of death? How can we act humanly in the midst of the Fall? *How shall we sing the Lord's song in a strange land?*—as the 137th Psalm, which I have used as an introit for this book, cries out. I bear the Book of Revelation as responsive to the question of the psalm.

If, then, there be those who find this tract cryptic, it will only be, I think, because it actually bespeaks a theology of hope at a time in America when death is so lively and familiar that death seems to be the only moral reality.

William Stringfellow

The Feast of Simeon Barsabba'e 1973
Block Island, Rhode Island

"Rejoice over her, O heaven,
O saints and apostles and prophets,
for God has given judgment for you against her!"

Then a mighty angel took up a stone like a great millstone
    and threw it into the sea, saying,

"So shall Babylon the great city be thrown down with
    violence,
    and shall be found no more;
and the sound of harpers and minstrels, of flute players
    and trumpeters,
    shall be heard in thee no more;
and a craftsman of any craft
    shall be found in thee no more;
and the sound of the millstone
    shall be heard in thee no more;
and the light of a lamp
    shall shine in thee no more;
and the voice of bridegroom and bride
    shall be heard in thee no more;
for thy merchants were the great men of the earth,
    and all nations were deceived by thy sorcery.

And in her was found the blood of prophets and of saints,
    and of all who have been slain on earth."

Revelation 18:20–24

chapter one

The Relevance of Babylon

One of the peculiar insights of the Book of Revelation—that most curious, most neglected part of the Bible—is that the doom of Babylon, the great city, occasions a celebration in heaven.

The scene, as depicted in the biblical images, does not seem to be one appropriate to rejoicing. The once mighty city is laid waste. Everything is despoiled. It has become a place haunted by death. Judgment has happened. Even the dirge of the kings and merchants of the earth over the fall of Babylon has finished. The great city can be found no more. There is such desolation that silence is all that is left (Rev. 18).

It is at *this* that "the voice of a great multitude in heaven" cries "Hallelujah!" and sings a hymn of triumph (Rev. 19:1).

How odd, as it seems to us, that the death of a society—especially, perhaps, the violent disintegration of this most rich and most powerful of all nations: Babylon—should incite jubilation in heaven.

If you examine the Babylon texts in Revelation, you will

26   **An Ethic**
**for Christians and Other Aliens
in a Strange Land**

find that the song of the heavenly chorus is punctuated by a
refrain, repeated three times, each in different words:

> Hallelujah! Salvation and glory and power belong to our God, . . .
> Hallelujah! The smoke [of Babylon] goes up for ever and
> ever. . . .
> Hallelujah! For the Lord our God the Almighty reigns (Rev.
> 19:1, 3, 6).

Odd, indeed! These various refrains are, in their biblical
context, interchangeable; they each express the same meaning. They are, literally, refrains, in which the destruction
of the nation is, somehow, associated with the salvation of
the world and in which Babylon's doom is accounted as a
sign of the sovereignty of God over nations and over humans (Rev. 15:3–4; 16:5–7; 18:6–8; 18:19–20).

Revelation as Ethics

It is a pity that Americans have been so recalcitrant toward the Bible, for all the contrary pretenses in the country's public rituals and despite the grandiose religiosity in
America concerning the familiar fictions about the nation's
destiny. It is specifically a misfortune, it seems to me, that
most Americans, whether or not they keep a church connection, are either ignorant or obtuse about Revelation and
the issues which the book raises in its Babylon passages. Had
the American inheritance been different, had Americans
been far less religiose and much more biblical, had the
American experience as a nation not been so Babylonian,
we might have been edified—in a fearful and marvelous and
timely way—by this biblical witness, and Americans might
be in more hopeful and more happy circumstances today.

Instead, Americans for the most part have dismissed the
Bible as apolitical—a private witness shrouded in holy neu-
trality so far as politics is concerned, having nothing beyond
vague and innocuous exhortation to do with the nation as
such, relegated to the peripheries of social conflict. Thereby
Americans have actually suppressed the Bible, since the

Revelation as Ethics

Bible is *essentially* political, having to do with the fulfillment of humanity in society or, in traditional words, with
the saga of salvation.

The treatment of the particular book of the Bible which I
cite here, the Revelation to John, is the striking illustration
at point. We have deemed it esoteric poetry, to be put aside
as inherently obscure and impractical by definition; or we
have regarded it, somewhat apprehensively, as a diary of
psychedelic visions inappropriately appended to the rest of
Scripture; or else we have suffered the arrogant pietism of
itinerant evangelists preaching a quaint damnation from
fragments of the book and acquiesced to their boast that *that*
is what Revelation is about. Some have demeaned the whole
of the Bible by distorting this book as a predestinarian
chronicle. Seldom is the specific political use to which the
book was put in its original context in the first century even
mentioned in church or known to contemporary church folk.
Most often, I observe, Americans, including the professed
Christians and the habituated churchgoers, have just been
wholly indifferent to Revelation.

Whatever reasons can be assigned for it, Americans fail
to comprehend Revelation as an ethical literature concerning
the character and timeliness of God's judgment, not only of
persons, but over nations and, in truth, over all principalities and powers—which is to say, all authorities,
corporations, institutions, traditions, processes, structures,
bureaucracies, ideologies, systems, sciences, and the like. As
such—except for the accounts of the Crucifixion of Jesus
Christ in the Gospels—Revelation is manifestly the most
political part of the New Testament.

The Demoralization of America

If this be so, it is both a significant evidence and partial
explanation of America's moral incapacitation or moral impoverishment, nowadays so ubiquitous and ominous, of
which all citizens partake, although, as with so much else
in this country, not equally:

28   **An Ethic**
for Christians and Other Aliens
in a Strange Land

- Moral poverty threatens, for instance, the prosperous more than the economically deprived because the affluent have more at risk, both materially and psychically, in *any* social crisis.

- Moral incapacity, similarly, afflicts the middle-aged more than the young because they have existed longer in conformity and do not have enough time left to change—even if they could discern how to change.

- Moral poverty is more virulent among whites than among blacks or Indians or Chicanos because the lives and livelihoods of most American whites have been subsidized by racial privilege for more than three hundred and fifty years on this continent, and white Americans are not about to allow that to be upset.

- Moral impoverishment is a larger burden for those in nominal leadership—as well as those actually in power —in the ruling institutions of society than it is to those who remain unorganized, unrepresented, unheeded, powerless, or, seemingly, hapless victims of the status quo, because the incumbents in power and the so-called leaders of the nation are located where social renewal must be generated.

- And—as if it required mention—moral poverty is most insidious and most notorious in exactly the precincts where moral sensibility is most pathetically needed at this moment: among those who exercise the authority of the State, prosecutors and policemen as much as judges and cabinet attachés. Most of all, it is needed in the Presidency, as compared, say, to defendants in political trials or those vulnerable to preventive detention or those murdered under a guise of legality or those driven into exile or those whose lives are squandered in vainglorious war. It is so desperately needed precisely because the *only* moral authority of the State is that which is disclosed as its last authority, which is death.

The Demoralization of America

Notice, please, that the penury, in a moral sense, which beleaguers so severely Americans of privilege, affluence, power or similar vested interest in the inherited and established order—and which affects all citizens, in one way or another, of whatever fate or fortune in the status quo—is not the same concern as imputing malignity to the middle classes or the middle-aged or the whites or the institutional hierarchies or those in political office. God knows (it is God's vocation, not any man's work and not any institution's function, to exercise such knowledge), America has wicked men in high places. It may be that there is a reciprocal relationship between villainy or personal immorality and conventional success in this society, but that is not the issue immediately raised in emphasizing the nation's moral poverty. Conceding a maximum efficacy to human wickedness comes nowhere near accounting for America's moral crisis. More than that, the same is not consistent with the biblical comprehension of moral issues affecting either institutions (including nations) or human beings. That is why I have said Americans might have been enlightened about their present moral situation, corporately and individually, had they been more biblically intelligent.

I mean by "moral impoverishment" what the Bible often cites as "hardness of the heart" or as the impairment or loss of moral discernment; the incapacity to hear, though one has ears; or to see, though one has eyes (e.g., Mark 8:14–21). I refer, thus, not so much to an evil mind as to a paralyzed conscience; not so much to either personal or corporate immorality as to a social pathology possessing persons and institutions; not so much to malevolence, however incarnate, as to the literal demoralization of human life in society.

If there be evildoers in the Pentagon or on Wall Street or in prosecutors' offices or among university trustees and administrators or in the CIA or on Madison Avenue or in the FBI or in the ecclesiastical hierarchies or in the cabinet (it would be utterly astonishing if there were not), that is not as morally significant as the occupation of these same and similar premises by men who have become captive and

30   An Ethic
for Christians and Other Aliens
in a Strange Land

immobilized as human beings by their habitual obeisance to institutions or other principalities as idols. These are persons who have become so entrapped in tradition, or, often, mere routine, who are so fascinated by institutional machinations, who are so much in bondage to the cause of preserving the principality oblivious to the consequences and costs either for other human beings or themselves that they have been thwarted in their moral development. Deprived of moral insight, they are impaired in the elemental capacity which distinguishes humans from other creatures. To furnish definite examples, I refer to those public officials and corporate figures who, during more than a decade now, have denounced reason and conscience by naming each escalation and re-escalation of war a way to quicken peace; or those who mention the ecological crisis but advocate, in the same breath, unrestricted expansion of the very elements of the American economy which have been proved to be most harmful to life; or those who nominally praise the rule of law but dishonor the Bill of Rights amendments by authorizing the defamation and repression of citizens who dare utilize their constitutional rights.

However many evil men hold places in the American establishment, they are far, far outnumbered, by my tally, by those bereft of conscience, so pathetically have they been dehumanized by the principalities and powers for which they are acolytes. And if the moral problem on such supposedly exalted levels of society is not so much wicked men as morally retarded men, then think of the cruel and somber daily existence of the multitudes of automatons of lower status and lesser privilege. They do not even have an illusion of power, the condiments of office, important reputation, or real wealth to insulate or console themselves from the imperious and obdurate totalitarian claims of the principalities against human life in society. For these folk, ridiculed on all sides (though most pointedly by their erstwhile champions) as "the silent majority," the American institutional and ideological ethos incubates a profound apathy toward human life as such. For them, the American experi-

The Demoralization of America

ence induces a fearful obstinance toward their own most elementary self-interest as human beings, not to mention an inbred indifference to human freedom. Again and again, the latter materializes as a default toward the humanity of others morally equivalent to hostility toward other persons and to enmity for mankind. Somehow, the American bourgeoisie are nurtured and conformed in a manner that results in a strange and terrible quitting as human beings.

For these Americans, I suggest it is not so much that they are duped by official deceit or brainwashed by official falsehood—although it is the truth that they are—as that they have been stupefied as human beings, individually and as a class of persons, and thus relieved of moral sanity. How else can the prolonged acquiescence of the majority to the squander, deception, corruption, aggression, and barbarism in Indochina be explained? Or, for that matter, how else can the continued manipulation of white racism among the American majority classes—as in the elaborate charade about school busing or in the Presidential assault upon welfare recipients—be understood? From such a reign of death—as Saint Paul would have named it—there are by now only such apparent respites or escapes as commercial sports and entertainments, booze, indulgence in nostalgia for a fictional past, a spectator role at moonshots or at heavily staged appearances of the President, the anxious diversions occasioned by inflation and indebtedness, and a place in the audience at officially contrived and sanctioned persecutions of those citizens who are still not conformed.

It goes without saying, in my view, that in circumstances where moral decadence in the sense meant here becomes so pervasive in a nation, one can discern and identify maturity, conscience, and, paradoxically, freedom in human beings *only* among those who are in conflict with the established order—those who are opponents of the status quo, those in rebellion against the system, those who are prisoners, resisters, fugitives, and victims. And only, by the same token, incidentally, can one postulate any ground of hope for a viable future for the United States.

32

**An Ethic
for Christians and Other Aliens
in a Strange Land**

Babylon as Parable

The failure of conscience in American society among its reputed leaders, the deep-seated contempt for human life among the managers of society, the moral deprivation of so-called middle Americans resembles, as has been observed, the estate described biblically as "hardness of the heart." This same condition, afflicting both individuals and institutions (including nations) is otherwise designated in the Bible as a form of demonic possession (Luke 8:9–15; cf. Matt. 16:21–28; Mark 8:14–31, 9:19–25).

If that seems a quaint allusion, more or less meaningless in modern times, keep in mind that *demonic* refers to death comprehended as a moral reality. Hence, for a man to be "possessed of a demon" means concretely that he is a captive of the power of death in one or another of the manifestations which death assumes in history. Physical or mental illnesses are frequent and familiar examples, but the moral impairment of a person (as where the conscience has been retarded or intimidated) is an instance of demonic possession, too. In a somewhat similar way, a nation, or any other principality, may be such a dehumanizing influence with respect to human life in society, may be of such antihuman purpose and policy, may pursue such a course which so demeans human life and so profits death that it must be said, analytically as well as metaphorically, that that nation or other principality is in truth governed by the power of death.

The spectacular example, in the earlier part of the twentieth century, of a nation and society and its majority classes and its leaders existing in precisely this condition is, of course, Nazi Germany.

The biblical story of such a realm is the saga of Babylon.

The extraordinary instance in the present time of the same situation is the United States of America.

That is not to say, please remember, that Nazi Germany and emergent contemporary American totalitarianism are identical. There are, unhappily, significant and literally ominous comparisons that are warranted between the two. But there are distinctions of importance too that argue against too hasty or oversimple equation of one with the other. (For one thing, the ideological element so conspicuous in Nazi totalitarianism is, to an appreciable extent, displaced by technological methodism in the gathering American totalitarianism.)

What I do say is that Babylon represents the essential version of the demonic in triumph in a nation. Babylon is thus a parable for Nazi Germany. And Babylon is thus a parable for America. In *that* way, there is an inherent and idiopathic connection between the Nazi estate in the thirties and what is now happening in America.

I do not, by the way, overlook a sense in which the biblical witness in the Babylon material in Revelation may be regarded as an apocalyptic parable having cosmic as well as historic relevance. On the contrary, within the sphere of apocalyptic insight, the Babylon epic bespeaks the moral character of *every* nation and of every other principality which is or which was or which may be. At the moment, however, I am deliberately putting this emphasis in the background, lest anyone embrace it as an excuse to play down or gainsay the specific relevance of Babylon for the contemporary American experience.

The risk in so treating the Babylon adventure is that some will conclude that these times in America are apocalyptic and then hasten on to confuse an American apocalypse with *the Apocalypse.* Well, these are apocalyptic days for America, I believe, but an American apocalypse is not likely to be the terminal event of history. To indulge this confusion is, I think, an inverse and perverse form of the same vanity in which the "American dream" or the popular mythology concerning a unique destiny of the American nation has come to so many, many Americans to mean grandiose visions of paradise found.

Americans of all sorts, of every faction and each generation, have by now suffered enough the consequences—which

34   An Ethic
                    for Christians and Other Aliens
                         in a Strange Land

only glorify death—of ridiculous national vanity and of the
truly incredible theological naïveté and moral incapacity
from which it issues.

My concern is for the exorcism of that vain spirit. My plea
is for freedom from this awful naïveté and for healing from
this moral flaw. My hope, therefore, as a human being,
begins in the truth that America *is* Babylon.

Biblical Faith and Pagan Idolatries

Two societies are prominent in the biblical witness. There
is Babylon, and there is also Jerusalem.

Babylon is the city of death, Jerusalem is the city of
salvation; Babylon, the dominion of alienation, babel,
slavery, war, Jerusalem, the community of reconciliation,
sanity, freedom, peace; Babylon, the harlot, Jerusalem, the
bride of God; Babylon, the realm of demons and foul spirits,
Jerusalem, the dwelling place in which all creatures are
fulfilled; Babylon, an abomination to the Lord, Jerusalem,
the holy nation; Babylon, doomed, Jerusalem, redeemed.

In these diametrically contrasted images of society, biblical
faith (both Judaism and Christianity) is generically distinguished from philosophies, ideologies, and religions (like
Platonism, Marxism, Buddhism) in which some singular
conception of society perfected is offered as a hypothetical
or idealistic or mythological tenet. Whatever else supplies
differences among these pagan (that is, nonbiblical) views,
they share a characteristic of projecting an idea of society
in vacuo, whether it be an extrahistorical abstraction or a
pseudohistorical destination or a posthistorical vision which
is posed against the empirical existence of actual nations in
history. Utopia literally means "no place," while the "dic-
tatorship of the proletariat" is—empirically speaking—an
illusion, and Nirvana denominates oblivion.

It neither denies nor diminishes the potency of any of
these positions—or their legion derivatives, variations, versions, or sects—to notice that all have an otherworldly or

Biblical Faith and Pagan Idolatries

nonworldly orientation. Each looks beyond time; each reaches outside common history; indeed, each departs from the categories of time and history to posit an idea or an ideal or an idyll of society. In relation to the world as it is, in the everyday existence and activity of principalities, nations, and human beings, each establishes similar arbitrary and artificial polarities between lofty concept and realpolitik, between what ought to be and what is, between vision or thesis or dream and actuality.

What disputes might be had on the comparative merit or appeal of any of these positions, or any of their factions or counterparts, are of little interest here. What occasions a nation or institution to become fascinated with and beholden to a particular philosophy or ideology or religion is not of immediate concern. What impels a person to embrace and advocate one or another of these schemata as offering either ultimate meanings or mundane efficacy for either oneself or humanity at large is not the present problem. Whether or not for a principality, such as a nation or a corporation, or for a human being, the entire issue of religious or ideological or philosophical adherence is in truth a delusion or contrivance or rationalization begetting, if disguising, an idolatry of death as a moral power is for the moment deferred. The nonbiblical faiths are cited only to underscore how biblical faith in the Old Testament and in the New Covenant is differentiated from them and how that is significant for social ethics and for politics. I am neither saying nor hinting that biblical faith is utterly incomparable with these other traditions, as pharisees sometimes argue. I am making no arrogant claims for biblical faith; according to the Bible there is no need for that (James 1:5–21; cf. Rom. 1:20–23). I do not suppose, in other words, that revelation is unrelated to human insight or, for that matter, to institutional wisdom. All that I do insist upon is that, if biblical faith is to be edifying to human beings, today or in any day, in America or in any society, the Bible must be respected for its own integrity and characteristics. Any approach to

36   An Ethic
                                    for Christians and Other Aliens
                                    in a Strange Land

the biblical witness must not be prejudiced or reduced or otherwise gratuitously distorted by casual or indiscriminate classification with philosophy or ideology or religion.

Hence, whatever may be said which relates biblical faith and the pagan idolatries, the former remains distinguished from each and all of the latter because it proposes no other-worldly conception of perfected society. It projects no extra-historical social vision; it does not abstract the issue of society from the condition of time. On the contrary, biblical faith merely concentrates upon events as they happen in the world as it is. Biblical faith focuses upon societal realities of every description as they exist in time; biblical faith is concerned with *this* world realistically; biblical faith is wrought within the human situation as human beings experience it, and within the historic circumstances of living nations. In contrast to hypothetical or idealized or mythological propositions of philosophy or ideology or religion, biblical faith thus possesses an essentially empirical orientation. It comprehends the ongoing history of human beings and principalities as it is taking place. It encompasses the common existence of persons and nations in time, and contemplates no destiny for any humans or for any institutions or similar creatures beyond familiar history or outside of time.

This peculiar empiricism of the biblical witness has certain elementary implications for social ethics and tactics. The unempirical or otherworldly context of any of the non-biblical views, in practice, means they despair of life in this world. They are fatalistic or myopic or otherwise naïve about the moral reality of death in this world, and they are incapacitated in confronting the power of death at work in the world, that is, in facing the fallenness of humans and institutions. In one way or another, *as a matter of principle,* they each renounce time as the era of creation and regeneration, negate history as the redemptive realm, reject or abandon this world.

Biblical faith, in contrast, acknowledges, describes, and

Biblical Faith and Pagan Idolatries

reports the fallenness of time and history. Biblical faith discerns the ubiquity and moral potency of death but bespeaks the recurrent transcendence of time within time, the transfiguration of common history, the sacramentalization of life for persons, for nations, for all creatures in this world so long as this world lasts. In short, unlike the pagan faiths —whatever merits they may nevertheless boast—the biblical Word beholds and affirms this time and this place and all experience in this world, fallen as it is, as coincidentally the subject of God's sovereignty, of his concern and of his incessant activity.

Then I heard another voice from heaven saying,

"Come out of her, my people,
lest you take part in her sins,
lest you share in her plagues;
for her sins are heaped high as heaven,
and God has remembered her iniquities.
Render to her as she herself has rendered,
and repay her double for her deeds;
mix a double draught for her in the cup she mixed.
As she glorified herself and played the wanton,
so give her a like measure of torment and mourning.
Since in her heart she says, 'A queen I sit,
I am no widow, mourning I shall never see,'
so shall her plagues come in a single day,
pestilence and mourning and famine,
and she shall be burned with fire;
for mighty is the Lord God who judges her."

Revelation 18:4–8

chapter two

The Empirical Integrity of the Biblical Witness

The recognition and affirmation of the empirical integrity and vitality of biblical faith will, I trust, readily be recognized as standing within that venerable tradition in Christian confession and belief sometimes named incarnational theology. In the New Testament it is explicitly informed in the Gospel of John, in much of Saint Paul's writings, in the Letter to the Hebrews, in the Epistle of James, and elsewhere, and it is this tradition which is so curiously celebrated throughout the Book of Revelation.

Incarnational theology regards this world in the fullness of its fallen estate as *simultaneously* disclosing the ecumenical, militant, triumphant presence of God. It esteems that which is most characteristic of Jesus Christ as the incarnate Word of God as also inherent in the whole of Creation.

It is the incarnational aspect of biblical faith, with its exemplary affirmations about time and history, and with its radical and preemptive concern for life in this world, from which the viable ethics and political action of the gospel issue. *The biblical topic is politics,* as has been previously, more succinctly, mentioned. From this standpoint, if the social ethics of biblical faith are compared with those deduced or propositioned or projected in philosophy or ideology or religion, the latter are more accurately deemed antiethics.

The Incarnation as the Sanctification of the World

Of course I am cognizant of sentiments, particularly popularized within American Christendom, which dispute the incarnational significance of time and the incarnational integrity of history and thereby forfeit that which is most distinctive about the ethics and politics of the Bible. Such convictions imitate the nonempirical emphases of the pagan idolatries: they construe rejection of this world as the premise of the gospel and departure from this world as the hope of the gospel. Thus they magnify the power of death in this world. And I am aware of the facility with which apparent proof-texts can be excerpted to convenience these sentiments, including some references in the Bible to "heaven" or to "eternal life," or some eschatological allusions and certain remarks of Jesus, as when he declares that his kingship is "not of this world" (John 8:23).

I eschew games with proof-texts. The biblical Word is worthy of a better attention than manipulative verbal gamesmanship, however piously motivated. At the same time, I do not burden this tract to digress into much of what might be said to expound and commend incarnational interpretations of time and history as typically biblical and, in turn, to sanction and explicate incarnational or sacramental social ethics. Still, many American churchfolk *do* repudiate this world as the basic article of their professed Christianity. I pause enough to mention therefore that the elemental issue involved here is the comprehension of Jesus Christ in that aspect which is most decisive and most interesting for human beings, as well as for the principalities, namely, Christ's relationship to the life of this world *in* this

The Incarnation as the Sanctification of the World

world. There are those within Christendom who are inclined to narrowly define or virtually ignore or even deny the meaning of the incarnation in Christ for the whole of existence in this world, while extolling "heaven" or "hereafter." They are thus challenging not only the first chapter of the Gospel of Saint John, but also the repetitive tenor of the New Testament witness which esteems Christ as embodying, exemplifying, and verifying the Word of God in a way which reveals God's dominion over, affection for, and vitality in this world. In any sanctuaries—I fear there are many of them—where the preaching and teaching is about a fancied "afterlife" instead of this life; about some indefinite "hereafter" instead of the here and now; about immortality (which is actually an elaborate synonym for memory) instead of resurrection (which means living in emancipation from the power of death); about "heaven"— as if that name designates a destination in outer space— instead of participation in a moral estate or condition; or about "eternal life" as a negation of this life—instead of the temporal fulfillment of life: where these or similar doctrines prevail, there is patent distortion of what the author of Hebrews calls "the elementary doctrines of Christ" (Heb. 6:1–2). In these circumstances, Christ is no longer beheld as the Lord of time and history, as the sovereign of Creation, as the new Adam, as the Redeemer. Rather he is demeaned to become a nebulous, illusive, spiritualized figure, a sacred vagueness severed from his own historic ministry. Separated from human experience and bereft of living relationship with either history or the God of history, he is levitated out of time—though time be the *only* context, according to the Bible, in which humans have or have ever had any knowledge whatever of Christ.

So let it be plain that, as a biblical term, "heaven" is not a site in the galaxies any more than "hell" is located in the bowels of the earth. Rather it is that estate of self-knowledge and reconciliation and hope—that vocation, really; that blessedness—to which every human being and the whole of creation is called to live *here* in this world, aspires to live

44

**An Ethic
for Christians and Other Aliens
in a Strange Land**

here, and by the virtue of Christ is enabled to enter upon
here (Matt. 4:17–25; 5:20; 6:19–21). Similarly, biblically,
"eternal life" means the recognition of time as the redemptive era *now,* the affirmation of life in time without displacing
or distorting the reality of time *now,* the transcendence of
time within the everyday experience of time *now* (Matt. 27:
34–39; Luke 10:25–27; 18:18–22).

Again, the biblical eschatological references—usually
quaint, styled in language and imagery, often in parable,
associated with apocalyptic allusions—concern the consummation of this history not as some fantastic disjuncture but
as a happening profoundly implicated in the whole of the
history of this world (Mark 13:32–37; Luke 21:10–28). The
eschatological hope, biblically speaking, anticipates an end
of time which is, simultaneously, time's redemption. That
hope neither abolishes time nor repudiates the moral significance of time; on the contrary, the eschaton means the
moral completion or perfection of time. Moreover, the
biblical hope, eschatologically, is no disembodied abstraction, no ethereal notion, no antiworldly vision, but a hope
recurrently foreshadowed and empirically witnessed in
events taking place now, and all the time, in the common
history of persons and nations in this world.

It is exactly where the gospel is distorted so as to emulate
the nonempirical or otherworldly orientations of the pagan
alternatives that Christendom is most worldly. The focus of
the nonbiblical faiths—or of a corrupted Christianity imi-
tative of religion or ideology or philosophy—upon some
ideal, abstraction, or myth categorically severed from time
and history and, in principle, denouncing redemptive happenings in this world, represents an abdication of life in
this world for persons and principalities to the reign of
death. This kind of otherworldliness elevates death to ultimate preeminence as the moral reality of history and time.
It excludes God as a living presence (even though still hy-
pothetically entertaining assorted ideas of God) and, indeed,
negates life altogether. This otherworldliness is, paradoxically, the most worldly way; this otherworldliness or

The Incarnation as the Sanctification of the World

antiworldliness is actually conformity to the world with a vengeance. And, for professed Christians, it is the most ignominious possible apostasy.

The empirical distinction of biblical faith, as contrasted with the pagan idolatries, is, therefore, no pedantic quibble. It is the treatment of the biblical witness as if it were like a philosophy, ideology, or religion in the comprehension of this world in relation to the hope for society that has so frequently confounded the ethical wisdom and tactical activity of those persons and institutions professing Christianity. The biblical mind is not philosophic. Even less is it ideological. (If anything, it is antireligious.) But through the centuries there have been repeated temptations to categorize biblical faith in philosophical pigeonholes or to ideologize the gospel or to revert the Bible to mere religion and thus to captivate and conform the biblical witness to the world, that is to say, to the world in which—whether knowingly or not—death has been for a time ceded sovereignty or the place of God. The gospel accounts attest to this as a troublesome issue among the disciples of Jesus, and remarks of Jesus that his kingship is "not of this world" have concrete meaning in that context (cf. John 6:15; Matt. 26:53). The same became an anguished matter—sometimes inhibiting discernment and action—in the earliest congregations, as the Acts of the Apostles and some of Paul's letters to the Galatians and the Colossians show. It remained a contentious question throughout pre-Constantinian times. The Constantinian Arrangement, which has been the aegis of European and American Christendom ever since, apparently sublimated it but did not resolve it, and, if anything, caused conformance to the world to become an even more solemn problem.

The course of European and American Christendom since then has been scandalized by bizarre happenings: the Crusades, the Inquisition, the suppression of the Peasants' Revolt, the practice of genocide against North American Indians, the sanction of black chattel slavery in the United States, the opportune merger of white colonialism and the

46   **An Ethic**
for Christians and Other Aliens
in a Strange Land

missionary enterprise in the nineteenth century, the seduction and surrender of the churches to Nazism—to name only a very few. In this same chronicle belongs the stubborn, tortured, outrageous. churchly tradition of anti-Semitism.

Kierkegaard cautioned that the crisis for biblical faith concerning conformity to the world, in one form or another, occurs wherever the anomaly of an established church appears. In the United States, the Constantinian Accommodation has been marvelously proliferated. Practically all churches and sects are, in effect, established and, in turn, conformed to the dominant social philosophy or secular ideology or civic religion. Biblical faith, here, in consequence, is strenuously distorted and persistently ridiculed —in the name of God, of course.

Parenthetically, it is my own opinion that nobody should be quick or glad to condemn churches or churchmen of the previous generations or of other circumstances for often submitting to the world by forsaking or forfeiting the distinctive gender of the biblical witness. We should, I think, forbear blaming Constantine or Aquinas, so to speak, for the efforts of contemporary archpharisees to lend the name of Christ to the American war enterprise. After all, it is some kind of ironic acknowledgment of the fertility of the biblical ethic—and an inverse tribute to the militancy of the Holy Spirit in history—that there occur such grotesque distortions of the biblical Word, a paradox Saint Paul much appreciated (e.g., Rom. 1: 32; 2 Cor. 4: 8–12). Moreover, some of the confusions and compromises between biblical faith and prevalent philosophy, ideology, or religion stem from attempts of the churches to exercise an apologetic responsibility to the world or to practice a missionary vocation in the world. Zealous or benign motives do not, of course, purge or discount apostasy, but they should restrain others, whether inside or outside the churches, from eager or premature arrogance.

In any case, whatever the mode, extent, or frequency with which professed Christians as a society in history have been conformed to the world; however the biblical witness has,

The Incarnation as the Sanctification of the World

hence, been confused, suppressed, or otherwise importuned; something more is implicated in this persistent issue of conformance—against which so many predecessors in the gospel like Paul or Augustine or Kierkegaard or Bonhoeffer have disclaimed, complained, admonished, and withstood persecutions—than the acculturation of Christianity or an establishment of a church, the dilution of the biblical message or the abandonment of the mature vocation of Christians. Nor is the concern, here, particularly one of truth being endangered or exchanged for falsehoood, or of the good being compromised or corrupted by evil, or of the pure being defiled or adulterated. More is involved than pedantic distinctions, as interesting or as significant as they may be in how one conceives of the relationship of belief and society within the provinces of philosophy or ideology or religion on the one hand, or within the discipline of biblical faith on the other.

The sentiments of religion, ideological dogmas, the propositions of any philosophy are not anathema as such to biblical faith; rather, they are of a different species. They represent a pagan mentality which is alien and inappropriate to the Bible; they signal a life-style dissimilar to the biblical witness; they, in turn, prompt tactics essentially distinguishable from the action characteristic of biblical people. Whenever biblical faith is presumed to be of the same genre as these various other faiths—when, hence, the temptation is to conformance to the world in that sense— what comes to issue, what is challenged or contested, is the very genius of biblical knowledge: *the Bible deals with the sanctification of the actual history of nations and of human beings in this world as it is while that history is being lived.*

The Bible yields no ethics or ideas or virtues which are in and of themselves substantively superior in any sense to those asserted or sponsored by the pagan views. The unique aspect of biblical faith is that immediate, mundane history is beheld, affirmed, and lived as the true story of the redemption of time and Creation. Biblical ethics constitute a sacramental participation in history as it happens, transfiguring

48   An Ethic
                                   for Christians and Other Aliens
                                   in a Strange Land

the common existence of persons and principalities in this
world into the *only* history of salvation which there is for
humanity and all other creatures. In this saga, time is
transcended within the events of a single day—*today*—so
that all that is past, from the first day, is consummated and
all that may yet come, even unto the last day of this world,
is anticipated; so that today is esteemed in its real dignity,
as if it were the first day, as if it were the last day, as if it
were the only day, as if today and eternity were one.

In this story, there is no other place actually known to
human beings, except this world as it is—the place where
life is at once being lived; there are no other places for
which to search or yearn or hope—no utopia, no paradise,
no otherworldly afterlife; and no limbo, either.

In this history, in this time, Eden and the Fall, Jerusalem
and Babylon, Eschaton and Apocalypse converge here and
now.

Babylon and Jerusalem as Events

It is in connection with this peculiarity of biblical faith,
this unique comprehension of time and history in this world,
as distinguished from the myths, ideals, or hypotheses of
religion or ideology or philosophy, that the two societies of
the Bible—Babylon and Jerusalem—have specific significance.

To speak of the relevance of the Babylon passages in the
Book of Revelation as a parable for America in the seventies
or for Nazi Germany in the thirties—or, for that matter,
for any nation in any decade—recognizes the biblical Word
as an event in an esoteric sense. Babylon in Revelation is a
disclosure and description of an estate or condition which
corresponds to the empirical reality of each and every city—
of all societies—in history. The Babylon of Revelation is
archetypical of all nations.

The biblical witness in the Babylon episode is not a morbid hindsight into the decline and disintegration of a certain
ancient city in Central Mesopotamia. *That* Babylon had long

Babylon and Jerusalem as Events

since vanished from the earth by the time the Book of Revelation was uttered, and the visible "Babylon" contemporaneous with the Book was not the Babylonia of Mesopotamia but the Roman Empire under Domitian's reign. Thus the Word in Revelation is an event in an immediate way. But the Word also becomes event more than transiently, for more than the tenure of Domitian's regime, in that the essential character and authority of the Roman State at that particular time verifies the essential character and actual authority upon which any nation, and any regime in any nation, relies at any time in history.

By the same token, the Babylon of Revelation does not represent a predestinarian forecast, inevitably and automatically to be played out in due course like some cosmic horoscope, in violence to the creaturehood of both nations and humans and in travesty of the reputation of God as made known otherwise and elsewhere in the biblical testimony. To view the Babylon material in Revelation as mechanistic prophecy—or to treat any part of the Bible in such a fashion—is an extreme distortion of the prophetic ministry. It is in fact a contradiction of prophetic insight because it refutes the eventful predilection of the biblical Word. A construction of Revelation as foreordination denies in its full implication that either principalities or persons are living beings with identities of their own and with capabilities of decision and movement respected by God. And, in the end, such superstitions demean the vocation which the Gospels attribute to Jesus Christ, rendering him a quaint automaton, rather than the Son, of God.

This does not mean that the Babylon story in Revelation is of poetic status alone. This Babylon is allegorical of the condition of death reigning in each and every nation or similar principality. The fallenness of this same Babylon is empirically evident and, indeed, enacted everywhere, everyday, in the experience of specific nations. Thus the Word in the Babylon reference in Revelation is not abstract, but the Word is an event in that it concretely exposes and truthfully describes both the essential character and the particular

50

**An Ethic
for Christians and Other Aliens
in a Strange Land**

situation of a nation, and of all principalities in the world within the era of time. Babylon is the parable of the nation beheld in the manifold dimensions of the nation's actual, fallen existence in history. Babylon is—to put it most succinctly—the parable of the nation in the fullness of its apocalyptic reality.

The Word is event—in an esoteric or a discreet sense. That is, of course, the mark which distinguishes the whole biblical literature as contrasted with Greek thought or Marxist dogmatics or Buddhist introspections or with assorted sectarian or churchly disfigurements of the Bible. Do not mistake my appreciation for the empirical vitality of the biblical Word as literalism, however. Any literalistic interpretations of the Bible are a false pretense—a substitute for, rather than a type of exegesis—which violates by their verbatim mechanics the Bible's generic virtue as a living testament. They devalue the humanity of the reader or listener by assigning the person a narrow and passive role depleted of the dignity of participation in encounter with the biblical Word which the vitality of that Word itself at once invites and teaches.

The relevance of Babylon as a parable of the fallen nation in the maturity of its apocalyptic destiny stands in counterpoint to the significance of the other biblical nation, Jerusalem. What Babylon means theologically and, hence, existentially for all nations or other principalities in the dimensions of fallenness, doom, and death, Jerusalem means to each nation or power in the terms of holiness, redemption, and life. Babylon describes the apocalyptic while Jerusalem embodies the eschatological as these two realities become recognizable in the present, common history of the world.

I am not implying that there is a neat parallelism in the manner in which Babylon on the one hand and Jerusalem on the other relate to the nations and institutions or to the practical situation of any particular principality. The interplay of Babylon and Jerusalem is dynamic and ironic and poignant, and it is specific as to each and every nation and power. Any description is inevitably too simplified, any analytical statement is insufficient. But, at least for now, it is enlightening to notice the paradoxical and the dialectical aspect of this interplay. The elementary truth of Babylon's apocalyptic situation is Babylon's radical confusion concerning her own identity and, in turn, her relationship to Jerusalem. The awful ambiguity of Babylon's fallenness is expressed consummately in Babylon's delusion that she is, or is becoming, Jerusalem. This is the same moral confusion which all principalities suffer in one way or another; this is the vocational crisis, really, which every nation in history endures. This is the vanity of every principality—and notably for a nation—that the principality is sovereign in history; which is to say, that it presumes it is the power in relation to which the moral significance of everything and everyone else is determined. Babylon's famous wantonness, Babylon's decadence, Babylon's profligacy has only most superficially to do with materialism, lust, or the decline of moral values, and Babylon's fall is not particularly a punishment for her greed or vice or aggrandizement, despite what some preachers allege. Babylon's futility is her idolatry—her boast of justifying significance or moral ultimacy in her destiny, her reputation, her capabilities, her authority, her glory as a nation. The moral pretenses of Imperial Rome, the millennial claims of Nazism, the arrogance of Marxist dogma, the anxious insistence that America be "number one" among nations are all versions of Babylon's idolatry. All share in this grandiose view of the nation by which the principality assumes the place of God in the world. In the doom of Babylon by the judgment of God this view is confounded and exposed, exhausted and extinguished. A magnificent celebration in heaven extols the triumph of God's sovereignty over principalities as well as human beings (Rev. 18:20; 19:1–2).

As every nation incarnates Babylon and imitates her idolatry, so each nation strives, vainly, to be or become Jerusalem. But, refuting and undoing that aim of nations, the reality of Jerusalem is *not* embodied in any nation or

52

**An Ethic
for Christians and Other Aliens
in a Strange Land**

other power. Jerusalem is the holy nation; Jerusalem is a separate nation. In the biblical image of Jerusalem and in the historic manifestations of Jerusalem as the priest of nations, Jerusalem lives within and outside the nations, alongside and over against the nations, coincident with but set apart from the nations. The emphatic tone in the Revelation passages in which the call "Come out [of Babylon], my people" is recited again and again points to this peculiar posture of simultaneous involvement and disassociation (Rev. 18: 4–5). It is pertinent to remember the prominence of this matter elsewhere in the New Testament. It was an issue, remember, which caused grave misunderstandings between Jesus and his disciples throughout his ministry. That is evidenced in their persistent bemusement at his parables, by their misapprehension of the Palm Sunday events, by their conduct at his arrest, by their mourning after the Crucifixion, by their surprise and consternation at Easter (i.e., Matt. 13; Mark 14:50; Luke 8:9–15, 19:28–44, 24:1–11; John 18:2–22). Only when Pentecost happens—where Israel is restored as a visible, viable, historic community and institution, as the holy nation—do the disciples and the others called into this new estate of humanity as society begin to comprehend the whereabouts of Jerusalem and Jerusalem's vocation among the nations (Acts 2:5–11, 36–47).

Babylon is concretely exemplified in the nations and the various other principalities—as in the Roman Empire, as in the U.S.A.—but Jerusalem is the parable for the Church of Jesus Christ, for the new or renewed Israel, for the priestly nation living both within and apart from the nations and powers of this world. Jerusalem is visibly exemplified as an embassy among the principalities—sometimes secretly, sometimes openly—or as a pioneer community—sometimes latently, sometimes notoriously—or as a prophetic society—sometimes discreetly, sometimes audaciously. And the life of Jerusalem, institutionalized in Christ's Church (which is never to be uncritically equated with ecclesiastical structures professing the name of the Church) is marvelously dynamic. Constantly changing in her appearances and forms, she is incessantly being rendered new, spontaneous, transcendent, paradoxical, improvised, radical, ecumenical, free.

In beholding some specific society or nation in history—like America—we must recognize the symbolic juxtaposition of the two biblical societies, Babylon and Jerusalem. Their contiguity signifies the convergence or confrontation or, indeed, collision of the apocalyptic and the eschatological events through which the past is consummated and the future is apprehended within the immediate scope and experience of that particular nation. It is in relation to these impending apocalyptic omens and imminent eschatological signs, in a time and in a place, that the body of the Church —and the person who is a Christian—decides and acts.

A Sacramental Ethic

Babylon!
Jerusalem!!
Apocalypse!!!
Eschaton!!!!

How do these names, these events, have practical consequence for the United States of America—or for any other principality—in the decade of the seventies? Daily the American nation is sorely beset by crises of fatal potential for both human life and institutional existence. And if that, indeed, suggests basic Babylonian similarities and invites apocalyptic descriptions, where in America is Jerusalem discerned? How can the eschatological hope be affirmed? What does hope mean ethically? Or politically?

On obvious, ominous, urgent fronts, society in America is right now desperately beleaguered by war and the entrenched commerce of war, by ecological corruption and the population problem, by profound racism and urban chaos, by technology and unemployability, by inflation and taxation. And all of these issues are compounded by unaccountability, secrecy, and practiced deception in government, by manifold threats to established authority and intimidating

54

**An Ethic
for Christians and Other Aliens
in a Strange Land**

official abuse of the rule of law, by vested intransigence to significant change and primary recourse to violence by agents of conformity and advocates of repression as well as some few professed revolutionaries. If a person looks to Revelation—especially its Babylon passages—as a political as much as theological tract at the time and in the circumstances in which it was uttered, is that of any help now, in this American situation? If, as is urged here, the biblical Babylon represents the essential estate of all nations and powers, verified empirically in the moral condition of any nation at any time in history, and if the biblical Jerusalem refers to Christ's Church in her vocation as the holy nation, standing apart from but ministering to the secular powers, how is that edifying to a Christian (or anyone else) who is today an American citizen? How must that concern him in decisions and conduct affecting allegiance to the nation, the claims of civil obedience, assent to prevalent social purposes, response to the pressures for conformity, participation in the rituals of national vanity, rendering honor to incumbent political authority, the prospects for reform or other change, the efficacy of protest, the tactics of resistance? Again, how does the biblical juxtaposition of Babylon and Jerusalem set a precedent for and inform the life-style and witness of the Church of Christ in America now? What do the ethics of biblical politics have to do concretely with the politics of the principalities and powers in America now?

To all such queries, biblical politics *categorically* furnish no answers.

The ethics of biblical politics offer no basis for divining specific, unambiguous, narrow, or ordained solutions for any social issue. Biblical theology does not deduce "the will of God" for political involvement or social action. The Bible— if it is esteemed for its own genius—does not yield "right" or "good" or "true" or "ultimate" answers. The Bible does not do that in seemingly private or personal matters; even less can it be said to do so in politics or institutional life.

This is not to say that biblical people, living on the contemporary scene in America or anywhere else, are thus

A Sacramental Ethic

consigned to holy ambivalence, well-intentioned indecision, or benign negligence in social crisis or public controversy. This does not counsel, comfort, or condone apathy, default, withdrawal, or any type of quietism (which, appearances to the contrary, are forms of political commitment, not options of abstension from politics). This does declare that the biblical witness affords no simplistic moral theology, no pietistic version of social ethics. Folk who yearn for the supposed reassurance of that kind of ethics can resort to the nation's civil religion or one of its legion equivalents; they will find no support or encouragement in the Bible.

The impotence of any scheme of ethics boasting answers of ultimate connotation or asserting the will of God is that time and history are not truly respected as the context of decision-making. Instead they are treated in an abstract, fragmented, selective, or otherwise, arbitrary version hung together at most under some illusory rubric of "progress," or "effectiveness," or "success." From a biblical vantage point as much as from an empirical outlook, this means a drastic incapacity to cope with history as the saga in which death as a moral power claims sovereignty over human beings and nations and all creatures. It means a failure to recognize time as the epoch of death's worldly reign, a misapprehension of the ubiquity of fallenness throughout the whole of Creation, and, in turn, a blindness to imminent and recurrent redemptive signs in the everyday life of this world.

Meanwhile, biblically speaking, the singular, straightforward issue of ethics—and the elementary topic of politics—is *how to live humanly during the Fall.* Any viable ethic—which is to say, any ethics worthy of human attention and practice, any ethics which manifest and verify hope —is both individual and social. It must deal with human decision and action in relation to the other creatures, notably the principalities and powers in the very midst of the conflict, distortion, alienation, disorientation, chaos, decadence of the Fall.

The ethics typically concocted from religion or ideology

56   **An Ethic
for Christians and Other Aliens
in a Strange Land**

or philosophy, including the Christianized, if unbiblical,
editions of the same, do not meet this necessity. In fact, they
repudiate time and common history as the sphere of ethical
concern and political action in multifarious ways. They may
focus upon asserted prospects beyond history, outside of
familiar time (like promises of afterlife or visions of a
hypothetical ideal society). They may deny the moral significance of time as the era of the Fall and diminish history
as the story of the Fall (as where imperial myths or doctrines of progress prevail). They may become literally
reactionary by reverting to nostalgia (as when the past, in
either fictional or factual variation, is posited as social model
or goal), or they may suffer no eschatological insight (being
oblivious to the possibility of human transcendence of time
within history) and remain, hence, radically irrelevant to
immediate mundane issues.

Biblical ethics do not pretend the social or political will
of God; biblical politics do not implement "right" or "ultimate" answers. In this world, the judgment of God remains
God's own secret. No creature is privy to it, and the task
of social ethics is not to second guess the judgment of God.

It is the inherent and redundant frustration of any pietistic
social ethics that the ethical question is presented as a
conundrum about the judgment of God in given circumstances. Human beings attempting to cope with *that* ethical
question are certain to be dehumanized. The Bible does not
pose any such riddles nor aspire to any such answers;
instead, in biblical context, such queries are transposed,
converted, rendered new. In the Bible, the ethical issue
becomes simply: *how can a person act humanly now?* Be
cautioned once more that by putting the ethical question so
starkly, no pretext is furnished for reading it as a private
or individualistic query. Indeed, the use of the adverb
humanly renders the question political; there is, in the
biblical witness, no way to act humanly in isolation from the
whole of humanity, no possibility for a person to act humanly without becoming implicated with all other human
beings.

A Sacramental Ethic

Let me state the same concern somewhat differently, in the context of biblical politics. Here the ethical question juxtaposes the witness of the holy nation—Jerusalem—to the other principalities, institutions and the other nations—as to which Babylon is a parable. It asks: *how can the Church of Jesus Christ celebrate human life in society now?*

I hope this manner of expressing the basic concern of social ethics, as posed biblically in contrast with various nonbiblical or pagan constructions, sufficiently emphasizes the vocational aspect of ethical decision and political action. The ethical wisdom of human beings cannot, and need not, imitate or preempt or displace the will of God, but is magnificently, unabashedly, and merely human. The ethical discernment of humans cannot anticipate and must not usurp the judgment of God, but is an existential event, an exercise of conscience—transient and fragile. To make such an affirmation and confession involves a radical reverence for the vocation of God and an equally radical acceptance of the vocation to be human. Moreover, it is the dignity of this ethical posture which frees human beings, in their decisions and tactics, to summon the powers and principalities, and similar creatures, to their vocation—the enhancement of human life in society (Gen. 1:20–31; cf. Mark 10:42–43).

Where Is Jerusalem?

Confronting the powers with their creaturehood—admonishing the principalities about their vocation as creatures called to serve the social need of human beings—is a requisite for Jerusalem. Such action can perhaps be most readily perceived in circumstances where the Church of Christ can be affirmed as the exemplary society or holy nation living in the midst of, yet set apart from, the nations and assorted principalities of the world: where Jerusalem is living juxtaposed with Babylon.

Yet surveying the contemporary churchly scene in the United States, one is much tempted to forego mention of the Church. Indeed, I notice that this is substantially what both

58

An Ethic
for Christians and Other Aliens
in a Strange Land

adherents of social gospel pietism and zealots of evangelical-ism have done while opting for, as they each do in their own ways, a supposed redemption by osmosis. I sympathize with their vain exaggerations of the efficacy of individualistic change and commitment, decision, and action. The Church, actually functioning as the ecumenical community or holy institution, is so hard to find or identify. If one speaks of Babylon, there is little hindrance in locating Babylon; it is not so very difficult to discern the Babylonian character of nations or other principalities. But if one bespeaks Jerusa-lem, as the new or renewed society of mature humanity, where is this Jerusalem? The answer cannot be in some spiritualized, spooky, sentimental conception of Church. The biblical precedents in the Old Testament witness and in Pentecost are not of some nebulous, ethereal, idealistic, otherworldly, or disembodied Church but of a visible, his-toric community and institution. They signal a new nation incarnating and sacramentalizing human life in society freed from bondage to the power of death. Where, nowadays, in America, is there such a Jerusalem reality of the Church?

It requires more bravado than I can muster to respond to this question by identifying *any* of the churches or sects or denominations or ecclesiastical principalities of the Ameri-can status quo with the Jerusalem aspect of the Church of Christ. In their practical existence, the familiar, inherited churchly institutions here bear little resemblance—even residually—to the Church as holy nation. In fact, some aboriginal American religions falsely impute the biblical vocation of the holy nation to America, in place of the Church of Christ. If Jerusalem and Babylon are each re-garded as parables, it is the Babylon image which is most apt for the conventional American churches—along with many other comparable powers within the precincts of Babylon, like the Pentagon (to name a rival bureaucracy), or the Mafia (to mention a rival in wealth), or the Teamsters Union (as an ethical rival). With these and similar princi-palities, the churchly enterprises are much engaged in elaborate worship of death. They are vainglorious about

Where Is Jerusalem?

reputation, status, prosperity, success; they are eager to conform, solicitous of patronage from the political regime, derisive of the biblical witness, accommodated to American culture. In fact, the American churchly institutions, for the most part, are not truly involved in apostasy—that is, in betraying the faith—or even in hypocrisy—that is, in practicing something other than what is preached. There can be no apostasy, if the faith has not been upheld; there can be no hypocrisy, if the gospel has not been preached.

The problem is more elementary and has to do with the specific cultural origins of so many of the American sects and denominations. It is not surprising to hear their propagation of the civic religion of the nation since their own traditions were generated in American culture, in Babylon, and not in Pentecost or in the subsequent biblical witness in history. So it is not that such "churches" have abandoned the gospel they once upheld and have become acculturated and conformed, but that they have been from their origins American cultural productions or Babylonian shrines.

I do not hereby dismiss categorically the whole of American Christendom. I do not suppose, either, that none of the churches on the American scene have memory of the biblical witness, because some do, notably the immigrant (as contrasted with the indigenous) churches. I do not conclude that no Christians can be found on churchly premises, including those which most blatantly are Babylonian shrines. I am saying that if you look for the Jerusalem reality of Church among the established ecclesiastical and churchly bodies, what you will find is chaos. Yet in the very same places, as well as elsewhere, can also be identified and affirmed some congregations and paracongregations, some happenings, some celebrations, some communities, some human beings who do suffer and enjoy the Jerusalem vocation in the midst of the chaos. The bizarre estate of the American churches does not mean, after all, that the Holy Spirit, so militant at Pentecost, has never visited America. Whether secreted within the established churches or detached from them, there lives in America a confessing movement—dy-

60   An Ethic
                         for Christians and Other Aliens
                               in a Strange Land

namic and erratic, spontaneous and radical, audacious and immature, committed if not altogether coherent, ecumenically open and often experimental, visible here and there and now and then, but unsettled institutionally, most of all—enacting a fearful hope for human life in society.

A specific instance of the emerging confessing movement in America can be found in the jails and prisons. In many of these, communities of mutual help and social concern have come into being and, among some prisoners, an intercessory witness, which is virtually monastic in character. What is taking place within prisons is deeply rooted in and informed by Bible study. The same is true of aspects of the confessing movement evident among young Christians such as the "Post-Americans." The charismatic renewal, immature though it yet may be, must also be comprehended within the reality of a confessing movement, along with some of the house churches or similar gatherings.

I have some hesitation, I must admit candidly, in using any name or term—like "confessing movement"—to refer to manifestations of the Jerusalem vocation of the Church. Naming any happening as Church tends to diminish the spontaneity and momentary character of the reality of the Jerusalem event in history. Or, to put the same concern differently, while Babylon represents the principality in bondage to death in time—and time is actually a form of *that* bondage—Jerusalem means the emancipation of human life in society from the rule of death and breaks through time, transcends time, anticipates within time the abolition of time. Thus the integrity or authenticity of the Jerusalem event in common history is always beheld as if it were a singular or momentary or unique happening. To be more concrete about it, if a congregation somewhere comes to life as Jerusalem at some hour, that carries no necessary implications for either the past or the future of that congregation. The Jerusalem occurrence is sufficient unto itself. There is—then and there—a transfiguration in which the momentary coincides with the eternal, the innocuous becomes momentous and the great is recognized as trivial, the end of history is revealed as the fulfillment of life here and now, and the whole of creation is beheld as sanctified.

So far as the human beings who are participants and witnesses in any manifestation of the Jerusalem reality of the Church are concerned, nothing similar may have happened before and nothing similar may happen again. But that does not detract from the event; it only emphasizes that the crux of the matter is the transcendence of time, rather than temporal continuity. This is why, obviously, I have earlier said that even though it becomes ludicrous to argue that the established churches in America represent Jerusalem, nevertheless—*here and there and now and then*—Jerusalem *is* apparent and militant on the scene of American Christendom. And, if it be any comfort, much the same thing must be said of the situation in earliest days of the Church, as the Book of the Acts of the Apostles verifies (Acts 15: 1–21; cf. Gal. 1:6–17, 2:1–10).

However chary it may be necessary to be about the whereabouts of Jerusalem both within and without the churchly status quo, it is not possible to avoid the issue, as individualistic dropouts and assorted purists and pietists are tempted to do. There is no unilateral, private, insulated, lonely, or eccentric Christian life. There is only the Christian as the member of the whole body; the Christian vocation for every single Christian is inherently ecumenical; the exclusive context of biblical ethics is biblical politics; even when a Christian acts apparently alone he does so as a surrogate for the Church; baptism signifies the public commitment of a person to humanity.

These are all expressions of the necessity of facing the question of how, concretely, the Jerusalem reality of the Church becomes manifest, from time to time and from place to place; these are various ways of affirming the corporateness of the Christian vocation and of emphasizing that ethical decisions and acts are essentially vocational—that is, they have to do with becoming and being human and not with guessing or imitating God's will. Of course, I include in this vocational designation of ethical conduct the exercise

62

**An Ethic
for Christians and Other Aliens
in a Strange Land**

of conscience, though I am mindful that conscientious witness is very often misconstrued as the most private and, even, idiosyncratic insight. The stereotypical response to an act of conscience is an accusation of arrogance by which someone who has done nothing denounces the conscientious for claiming moral superiority. That may be an appropriate construction of the nature and operation of conscience so far as the world is concerned, but it is not the biblical comprehension of conscience. Biblically, the exercise of conscience is not at all individualistic but the implementation of a person's elemental responsibility to human life, both one's own humanity and that of all others, as the famous commandment mentions (Matt. 22:34–40). It is not only not idiosyncratic, but rather the opposite, since the conscientious stand does not separate from but instead identifies with the common interest of human life. And the act of conscience is not inherently arrogant, as the conformed or the lazy or the fearful assert, because it strives not to approximate divine judgment but to represent mature human will.

There is a kind of confusion which prompts the thought that conscience is eccentric and arrogant rather than political and, actually, very humble—an enactment of the dual commandment, in fact. The principal reason for it is the false presupposition which frequently modifies ethical opinion that it is a necessity to be consistent and that a decision made today must be able to be rationalized in terms of prior actions, just as what may be determined tomorrow is narrowed to what can be logically or abstractly reconciled with what has been said and done today. This loyalty to consistency may be the way of the Greek mind, or of the American mentality, but it is alien to the biblical style. It may be apropos in philosophy, ideology, or, sometimes, religion, but it is not a feature of the gospel. It may contain morbid appeal for those professing Christianity who are nevertheless hung up in anxiety about their own justification, but consistency is no virtue for Christians. The ethical issue, whatever the particular existential circumstances, biblically speaking, concerns how to live, what to decide, how to act humanly in the midst of the Fall. That question occurs and recurs in every moment, and the response to it is always in each moment, imminent, and always breaking through the moment, transcendent. By dwelling upon the simultaneous imminence and transcendence of ethical decision, I do not gainsay experience or edification or maturation. In each of those senses, there is connection between the decisions and deeds of this day and the day before and the day to come (if it comes!!). But those relationships are not reduced to some blind adherence to consistency. Indeed, where such a rubric of consistency is imposed or assumed it is evidence of a drastic failure to take seriously the history of this world as the saga of the Fall and of a blindness to redemptive signs within that same saga. Where consistency prevails, the incarnational character of common history is ignored.

In biblical ethics, a Christian is implicated in merely but truly human decisions. These are unpredictable; extemporaneous; serious but not pretentious; conscientious but not presumptuous; dynamic and never immutable; historically serious and realistic and, hence, often inconsistent; momentary or imminent and yet transcendent, commonplace, and sacramental.

A Christian lives politically within time, on the scene of the Fall, as an alien in Babylon, in the midst of apocalyptic reality. Coincidentally, a biblical person lives politically, on the identical scene, as member and surrogate of Christ's Church, as a citizen of Jerusalem, the holy nation which is already and which is vouchsafed, during the eschatological event.

In ethical decision and in political action, in this world, a Christian is always, as it were, saying *no* and *yes* simultaneously.

A Christian says *no* to the power of death but in the same breath he bespeaks the authority of life freed from bondage to death. He exposes the reign of death in Babylon while affirming the aspiration for new life intuitive in all human beings and inherent in all principalities. He confounds the

64

**An Ethic
for Christians and Other Aliens
in a Strange Land**

wiles and stratagems of death by insistently, defiantly, resiliently living as no less and none other than a human being; he enjoins the works of death by living in human fulfillment now. He warns of the autonomy of God's judgment while rejoicing in the finality of God's mercy. He suffers whatever death can do as he celebrates the resurrection from death here and now.

One marvelous example of the biblical genius in discerning the ethical as the sacramental has, of course, been rendered at the outset of this book, in citing the jubilation of the heavenly chorus at Babylon's doom. The ethical question *what is to be done when the great city dies?* is answered in a sacramental way—*sing praise of the sovereignty of God over all nations.* In the event, the *no* which issues against death *is* at once the *yes* which celebrates life as a gift.

*After this I saw another angel coming
down from heaven, having great authority;
and the earth was made bright with his
splendor. And he called out with a mighty
voice,*

*"Fallen, fallen is Babylon the great!
It has become a dwelling place of demons,
a haunt of every foul spirit,
a haunt of every foul and hateful bird;
for all nations have drunk the wine of her
    impure passion,
and the kings of the earth have committed
    fornication with her,
and the merchants of the earth have grown
    rich with the wealth of her wantonness."*

Revelation 18:1–3

chapter three

The Moral Reality Named Death

The Babylon parable in the Book of Revelation ascribes death as the moral reality which rules nations and all other principalities and powers of this world (Rev. 12:7–12; 13:1–8). Death domineers these creatures. Death assumes for the principalities the office or role of God. Death permeates the whole of the existence of the principalities. Death is institutionalized in definite, identifiable forms in particular nations in specific circumstances; simultaneously, death is incarnate in the ethos of each nation, embodied in the traditions and aims of all the nations and powers.

In this world as it is, in the era of time, in common history—in the epoch of the Fall, as the Bible designates this scene—every value, every goal, every policy, every action, every routine, every enterprise of each and every principality has the elemental significance of death, notwithstanding any contrary appearances. This is eminently so with respect to nations, for nations are, as Revelation indicates, the archetypical principalities. All other assorted, diverse

68

**An Ethic
for Christians and Other Aliens
in a Strange Land**

principalities resemble them, imitate them, and substitute for them (Rev. 13:8–17; 14:8, 17).

All virtues which nations elevate and idolize—military prowess, material abundance, technological sophistication, imperial grandeur, high culture, racial pride, trade, prosperity, conquest, sport, language, or whatsoever—are ancillary and subservient to the moral presence of death in the nation. And it is the same with the surrogate nations —the other principalities, like the corporations and conglomerates, ideologies and bureaucracies, and authorities and institutions of every name and description.

After all is said and done, apart from God himself, death is the *only* extant moral power living in this world (notice Luke 10:17–20).

Death as Social Purpose

Now I am aware that some persons are inhibited from apprehending death as so powerful, so ubiquitous, so important a moral reality. Within American culture, there is a strenuous reluctance to admit death even at funerals. To the extent that death is customarily gainsaid within American society, it is not surprising that many people have difficulty in conceiving and speaking of death as a militant moral power as compared to the manner in which human beings usually think and talk of God. Indeed, it is an aspect of death's remarkable moral appeal, for both persons and principalities, that comprehension of death is so much beclouded. The efficaciousness of death as the preemptive idol in this world is occasioned, in part, by the deceptions and delusions which induce human beings, and nations, to underestimate death or misconstrue death, ignore death or, even, pretend that death does not exist.

This customary American denial of death as a visceral fact and the common oversight of death in its social implications have lately been modified by a growing fascination with the topic of death. It has surfaced in the so-called counterculture and, at the same time, in several American

Death as Social Purpose

subcultures, noticeably those of elderly citizens, of ghetto-ized blacks, of prison inmates, and of servicemen and Viet-nam veterans. In these subcultures, the banishment or abandonment of human beings to loneliness, isolation, ostra-cism, impoverishment, unemployability, separation—all of which are social forms of death—has become so dehumaniz-ing that the victims suffer few illusions about their consign-ment to death or to these moral equivalents of death by American society. In the counterculture, especially those disaffected offspring of the white bourgeoisie, the extraordi-nary proliferation of occult and pseudo-occult arts, or the escapades of the drug scene which parody the conventional death rituals of inherited culture, furnish evidence of spe-cific awareness of the moral sway of death in the nation.

Still, concerning death, there is much confusion and there are many timidities; there is too little lucidity and there is not too much coherence, so that the issue must be posed straightforwardly: *what does it mean to recognize death as a moral power?*

Let it be acknowledged that death is a mystery quite inexhaustible, as to which there will forever be more to notice, more to learn, more to say. Yet death is not utterly mysterious, and if, in speaking of death, there seem to be many innuendos, or if ambiguity is heightened, or if the name of death carries multiple allusions or diverse connota-tions, human beings are not bereft of insight or rendered inarticulate about death. The truth is that human beings are concerned with nothing else but death, though that be seldom realized. Thus, in this book, when the name of death is used, I intend that it bear *every* definition and nuance, *every* association and suggestion, *every* implication and intuition that *anyone* has *ever* attributed to death, and I intend that the name of death, here, bear all meanings simultaneously and cumulatively.

To be more concrete, death in the sense of biological termi-nation and death as defined in the efforts of the undertaker are both encompassed within the significance of death deemed a moral reality. These ordinary or vulgar designa-

70

An Ethic
for Christians and Other Aliens
in a Strange Land

tions or descriptions of death by no measure sufficiently explicate death's moral status, however. The name of death refers to clinical death and to biological extinction and includes the event of the undertaker, but, much more than that, the moral reality of death involves death comprehended sociologically and anthropologically, psychologically and psychically, economically and politically, societally and institutionally. Death as a moral power means death as social purpose.

A Grotesque Example

There are in the American experience as a nation—there are in any nation's story—literally numberless particular instances of death become social purpose. In America, however, there has been no more blunt, no more terrible apparition of the moral reality of death domineering the nation than the war in Indochina. In citing this peculiar war in order to elucidate death as a moral power, it is of elementary significance that the war in Southeast Asia represents a symptom of death incarnate in society and *not* the other way around. The war as symptomatic of death, rather than death being a symptom of the war, is the definitive moral fact.

There has been, it seems to me, during the past decade of the war, a confusion about just this point which, among other things, has frustrated much of the American opposition to the war. The notion has been widespread that the death purpose evident in the war could somehow be undone if the war could be ended. But that is as false as it is naïve; this Indochina war did not sponsor the moral power of death in American society. The war, rather, expresses, grotesquely, the moral presence of death which has *always* been in America, as in other principalities. And the end of the war promises no end, no diminishment even, to *that* presence.

One of the meanest deceptions of the political and military authorities has exploited this superficial view that the death purpose in America has only been a mark of the war

A Grotesque Example

by withdrawing and redeploying American troops in Southeast Asia so as to transfer casualties from the Americans to the Asians. Many Americans have thereby been induced to believe that the death element in the war was somehow reduced or removed since fewer Americans were dying. In fact, during the period of withdrawal the gross casualties among so-called allies and imputed enemies in Indochina, especially civilians, vastly increased. Empirically, death profited the more.

Meanwhile, if Americans have been importuned into supposing that the power of death has been diminished insofar as most of those killed in the war are Asians in place of Americans, complacency toward *other* symptoms of the moral reality of death in the nation has been encouraged. In popular version, the message propagated is that the war has somehow been the cause of whatever other social crises the nation suffers; hence, the apparent end of American troop participation in the war would resolve or mitigate those problems. The reality is that these great "social ills" have not been occasioned by the war, but, along with the war and interlaced with the war, they incarnate death in society. The status of the war, including whether it can truthfully be said to have ended, cannot affect that.

So if now I use the Indochina war as an example of death as social purpose in the nation, I am nevertheless mindful of many other symptoms of death in America—like the apartheid stalemate in race, the prevalent waste ethic in production and marketing and consumerism, the degeneration of medical care, the emergent technological totalitarianism, the militarization of the police power, the official assault against due process of law, and the proliferation of illegitimate authority. If one focuses upon the war in Southeast Asia to expose the relationship between death and society in America, it is not because that connection is uniquely disclosed in the war. It is as much evidenced in any of these other issues and would be so had there never been an American war in Indochina.

Manifestly, any war—war per se—is in immediate, physi-

72
An Ethic
for Christians and Other Aliens
in a Strange Land

cal, literal terms a tribute to death as ultimate virtue for a nation. At a very early stage in the Vietnam war, in an infamous incident, a field commander stated the death purpose succinctly, openly, and accurately when he observed after an operation that it had been necessary "to destroy this village in order to save it."

This war has been one in which the prevalent strategies betray this same, singular rationale of death: "protective reaction strike" means kill first and ask questions, if at all, later; "search and destroy" makes massacre a tactical concept; "body count" becomes the computation of "victory." These are policies and stratagems, in other words, which are genocidal *as a matter of principle.* Pentagon jargon is not ingenious enough to conceal that truth. In such a context, My Lai is no aberration but a direct implementation of the euphemistically stated strategic intent. And, in this same context, surely the hapless Lieutenant Calley would be a hero but for the expediency which rendered him a scapegoat for General Westmoreland and for others in the chain of command.

In a war which is genocidal in principle, no distinction is possible—pretense to the contrary—between military and civilian targets. The threatening of the North Vietnamese dikes, the napalming of hamlets, the defoliation of the earth, experiments in "weather warfare," the Christmas extermination bombardment in 1972 are so consistent with the death goal that they must be said to be deliberate.

The war in Indochina has been one in which the idolatry of death has acquired a curious sophistication through automation. "Smart bombs" and similar automated weapons have separated military personnel from visual or other physical contact with either an enemy or with civilian victims. This extraordinary change in warfare places military professionals and citizens back home in more nearly the same practical relationship to those who are being killed. And if it is tempting to suppose that remote proximity abolishes responsibility for the killing, it must be remembered that the use of apparently anonymous automated weapons exposes

A Grotesque Example

the common and equal culpability for slaughter of those who pull the trigger and those who press the button with those who manufacture the means and those who pay the taxes. The fact that a person does not see, and cannot foresee, the consequences of an action does not make the action either innocuous or innocent. Automated warfare, so sophisticated in Vietnam, dramatizes the corporate guilt of all Americans, civilian as much as serviceman, in the genocide of the war.

Throughout this war, the moral as well as physical presence of death has been accentuated in an extraordinary incidence of military professionalism of the most vain and self-serving sort. That military chauvinism has been accompanied by heavy emphasis upon the game aspect in war. Vietnam not only furnished pretext for wanton proliferation of Pentagon bureaucracy and its satellites in science, industry, public relations—with its boggling institutional redundancy, its radical material squander, and its wasting of human beings—but this war also has seen the most grandiose maneuvers conceivable. Any military doctrine or ploy or whim might be tried for the sake of the attempt alone; gadgets and weapons and systems could be field-tested just because they exist; technical capability to invent and experiment would be implemented without the interference of human discretion just because the capability is there. The usurpation of civilian control confessed by General Lavalle, the corruption of command responsibility exposed by Colonel Herbert and attested at My Lai, the machinations documented in *The Pentagon Papers,* the innumerable procurement scandals afford glimpses into how in this war death is unleashed against opposing armies or peasant victims or the environment itself and, at the same time, how death governs internally the American military principality and its corporate adjuncts.

That this has been a war without purpose—except death —explains why the only "allies" which the United States has had in it are mercenaries or puppets or criminal regimes in corrupting relationships literally like those of the Babylon parable (Rev. 18:3).

74   An Ethic
                                for Christians and Other Aliens
                                      in a Strange Land

For more than a decade of this war, death has so enthralled the leaders of the nation and so possessed the
nation's political, military, and intelligence institutions that
they have countenanced and abetted a drug traffic in Southeast Asia. Operated as patronage by ostensibly friendly
regimes, it has accounted for greater American casualties
than has combat. And that same purpose of death is further
verified in the official consignment of multitudes of veterans
of the war to disablement or illness, to unemployability and
to political harassment. For those who have been servicemen
in Vietnam, to have survived combat or the drug scene does
not mean to have eluded death, for death is ready, in these
other guises, for their return home.

In domestic society, during the war, death has been so
pervasive that few persons have failed to sense death's
vitality in America, in the compounding neglect of elementary human needs in shelter and education and work
and health and in so much more. In the relentless assaults
upon truth and reason and comprehension and conscience,
through omnipresent and seemingly omniscient surveillance,
by presumption of illegal authority, by the charades of
secrecy and deception, by the atmosphere created by official
babel, by the virtual abolition of credibility as a premise
and discipline of government: citizens are left anxious and
bewildered and numbed—dehumanized, or morally in a
condition of death.

These are some of the ways in which death enshrined as
social purpose in the nation can be described in terms of a
specific episode in the national experience—the war in
Southeast Asia. But do not conclude therefore that this war
has happened in a void or is somehow isolated from the rest
of the American story. The power of death militant in
America is neither unique to this nation (it is common to
all nations) nor novel in this war (it is a historic feature of
the nation from its origins). Morally, the "search and destroy" missions in Vietnam villages have their context in
the genocide practiced since the seventeenth century against
the American Indians. More immediately, the Indochina war

A Grotesque Example

in its most peculiar aspects was foreshadowed at Hiroshima. Hiroshima is the appropriate event and symbol (though others might be chosen) because when Hiroshima happened, that war—the Second World War—strategically and technically had already been won. Hiroshima, thus, represents a decisive triumph of self-serving technological capability joined with military professionalism, a nation's doing something essentially because it can be done. Hiroshima is the momentous, though not the first, instance of policy-making so dominated by technological facility as to be absorbed into the technical process. Hiroshima symbolizes devastation, destruction, obliteration for its own sake. Hiroshima means death as purpose for the nation.

Hiroshima, as a moral event, means that the spirit of death was victorious in the Second World War. All that has happened lately in Indochina effectuates, and embellishes, Hiroshima.

A Translation of the Fall

The estimation of death as a moral reality feigning sovereignty over Creation, the recognition of the Babylon reference in the Book of Revelation as a parable for nations and other principalities in their fallen status, the common idolatry of death in the United States, and the apocalyptic signs in the American experience as a nation are each versions of the biblical doctrine of the Fall.

I have a hesitation about pointing to this so directly. Someone could be misled into supposing that the generality and ubiquity of the fallenness of the whole of Creation somehow obviates attention to the reality of fallenness in particular circumstances. That all nations in the course of history are known to human beings in their fallen estate furnishes no extenuation from or mitigation of the reign of death—or of specific features of that reign—in America in the twentieth century. By much the same token, the appalling dimensions of alienation and brutality in Nazi Germany, for an example, do not diminish by an iota or in

76

**An Ethic
for Christians and Other Aliens
in a Strange Land**

any sense relieve the burden of the Fall in the U.S.A. Similarly, whatever the works of death of North Vietnam or of the Viet Cong, they have not rendered the American saturation bombings of civilians in North Vietnam less deadly or less atrocious, Pentagon morality to the contrary notwithstanding.

There simply is no way, either quantitatively or qualitatively, to assess or measure or compare fallenness. The only way to evaluate the moral power of death is as death.

My hesitancy in saying plainly that this book is, basically, some meditations on the biblical doctrine of the Fall is enlarged when I notice the distortions and perversions of the biblical view of the Fall that are so much propagated and popularized in this country. American pietism—both in the social gospel and in evangelicalism—is entranced with a notion that the Fall means the consequences of mere human sin, without significant reference to the fallen estate of the rest of Creation. And human sin, in turn, is—usually —quickly transposed into human willfulness or human selfishness or human pride—greed, duplicity, lust, dishonesty, malice, covetousness, depravity, and similar vices.

Yet human wickedness in this sense is so peripheral in the biblical version of the Fall that the pietistic interpretation that it represents the heart of the matter must be accounted gravely misleading. The biblical description of *the Fall concerns the alienation of the whole of Creation from God,* and, thus, the rupture and profound disorientation of all relationships within the whole of Creation. Human beings are fallen, indeed! But all other creatures suffer fallenness, too. And the other creatures include, as it were, not only cows, but corporations; the other creatures are, among others, the nations, the institutions, the principalities and powers. The biblical doctrine of the Fall means the brokenness of relationships among human beings and the other creatures, and the rest of Creation, and the spoiled or confused identity of each human being within herself or himself and each principality within itself. One can speak, appropriately, of human wickedness within the scope of the Fall, but only as an incidental matter within the time or history or era which the Fall designates, in which death apparently holds and exercises moral dominion over the whole of Creation.

Earlier it was said that ethics had to do with human decisions and conduct in relation to the principalities and powers in time. Now a reiteration is called for: ethics concerns human action in relation to the principalities and powers in the Fall, where both human beings and principalities, as well as the rest of Creation, exist under the claim that death is morally sovereign in history.

An ethics which ignores or omits the principalities, as American pietism traditionally has, and as the so-called social gospel practically has, is, biblically speaking, so deficient as to be either no ethics categorically or to be, as has been suggested, an antiethics.

Traits of the Principalities

The substantive questions here become: *Who or what are the principalities and powers? How are the principalities related to the moral reality of death?*

There are two sources of insight for these questions which complement and significantly verify one another. Those sources are the biblical references to the principalities and empirical observation of the principalities. It should be remembered, as to the latter, that detached scrutiny of the principalities by humans is not possible. The fundamental reality between persons and principalities is tension and strife, and such empirical perception as human beings may have is that of victim or intended victim of the principalities.

(1) the powers as legion

According to the Bible, the principalities are legion in species, number, variety, and name (e.g., Luke 8:29–33; Gal. 4:3; Eph. 1:21, 6:10–13; Col. 1:15–16, 2:10–23). They are

78   An Ethic
                                for Christians and Other Aliens
                                      in a Strange Land

designated by such multifarious titles as powers, virtues, thrones, authorities, dominions, demons, princes, strongholds, lords, angels, gods, elements, spirits. Sometimes the names of other creatures are appropriated for them, such as serpent, dragon, lion, beast. A similar practice survives today, of course, where animal symbols refer to nations or institutions: the bear is Russia, the tiger represents Princeton, the donkey the Democratic Party, the pig the police.

Terms which characterize are frequently used biblically in naming the principalities: "tempter," "mocker," "foul spirit," "destroyer," "adversary," "the enemy." And the privity of the principalities to the power of death incarnate is shown in mention of their agency to Beelzebub or Satan or the Devil or the Antichrist.

The very array of names and titles in biblical usage for the principalities and powers is some indication of the scope and significance of the subject for human beings. And if some of these seem quaint, transposed into contemporary language they lose quaintness and the principalities become recognizable and all too familiar: they include all institutions, all ideologies, all images, all movements, all causes, all corporations, all bureaucracies, all traditions, all methods and routines, all conglomerates, all races, all nations, all idols. Thus, the Pentagon or the Ford Motor Company or Harvard University or the Hudson Institute or Consolidated Edison or the Diners Club or the Olympics or the Methodist Church or the Teamsters Union are all principalities. So are capitalism, Maoism, humanism, Mormonism, astrology, the Puritan work ethic, science and scientism, white supremacy, patriotism plus many, many more—sports, sex, any profession or discipline, technology, money, the family—beyond any prospect of full enumeration. The principalities and powers *are* legion.

(2) the principalities as creatures

With these creatures, as with human beings, it is never quite possible to express either the whole personality or the

Traits of the Principalities

multiple attributes and abilities of a principality in a name, much less that of the legion of principalities and powers. The biblical practice of invoking many names or of interchanging various names, when speaking of principalities, is a help in grasping the many-faceted character and versatility of these powers. After all, what is being described and designated is a form of life, a creatureliness, which is potent and mobile and diverse, not static or neat or simply defined by what it may now or then be called. So such names as are used for the principalities, either in the biblical witness or in common talk, are necessarily suggestive, intuitive, emphatic.

A recurrent stumbling block to comprehending the principalities exists, for many people, at just this point. Human beings are reluctant to acknowledge institutions—or any of the other principalities—as creatures having their own existence, personality, and mode of life. Yet the Bible consistently speaks of the principalities as creatures. For another instance, the law (itself a principality) contains a similar recognition when it deals with various attributes of corporations, including corporate personality or existence in perpetuity or separate liability (i.e., Rev. 13).

The typical version of human reluctance to accord the principalities their due integrity as creatures is the illusion of human beings that they make or create and, hence, control institutions and that institutions are no more than groups of human beings duly organized. How do these creatures called principalities come into existence? How does an institution originate? Where does tradition come from? When is a nation born? How is an ideology created?

I am frank to admit no full answers to such queries and further to confess that I am more or less content to leave these questions unanswered. The exact origins of the creatureliness of principalities is a mystery in quite the same sense that the creaturehood of human beings remains mysterious. Within such mysteries, we are not bereft of any insight, but what is knowable is partial and ambiguous, limited and fragile. Thus, we know that human beings are privy to the public inception and generation of institutions

80   **An Ethic**
for Christians and Other Aliens
in a Strange Land

and other principalities. (In the time which has come to be
regarded as the birth of this nation, some men convened
and consulted and acted in concert.) Yet that human privity
seems insufficient to be the whole truth; something more
than the summation of human thought and activity is involved in the creature identity of principalities.

Perhaps the issue is put, with more edification, the other
way around: concerted or collective human action is, in and
of itself, too simple and transient to support the view that
principalities are creatures made by men. The creaturely
status of the principalities—on the contrary—comes not
from men, but from God. If that leaves, still, a large mystery,
it nevertheless emphasizes that all creatures are God's
creatures, that the creaturehood of principalities is essentially similar to that of human beings and is no more the
handiwork of men than human life is. And, moreover, an
understanding of the life of principalities as part of God's
work of creation, and not man's doing, is the biblical view
confirmed empirically by the most widespread redundant and
cumulative evidence that human beings do not control institutions or any other principalities.

(3) the fallenness of the principalities

The principalities are numbered among God's creatures,
yet they suffer the Fall as truly as human beings, as fully as
the rest of Creation. It is not that there are no perfect or
perfectable institutions (though there are none), but rather
that all institutions exist, in time, in a moral state which is
the equivalent of death or which has the meaning of death.
Every principality in its fallenness exists in remarkable
confusion as to its own origins, identity, and office. The
fallen principalities falsely—and futilely—claim autonomy
from God and dominion over human beings and the rest of
creation, thus disrupting and usurping the godly vocation or
blaspheming, while repudiating their own vocation. This is
apparent in every principality, but it is especially manifest
in great ideologies like Marxism or capitalism, or in rich

Traits of the Principalities

and powerful nations or empires, as in the Babylon parable, which often are quite literal in their preemption of God by their demands for obeisance, service, and glorification from human beings (Rev. 13:1–6).

The hostility of the fallen principalities and powers toward God and the profound confusion as to their own creatureliness which that rejection of God betrays issue in relentless aggression against all of life and, since the concern here is for ethics, especially aggression against human life in society. The principality, insinuating itself in the place of God, deceives humans into thinking and acting as if the moral worth or justification of human beings is defined and determined by commitment or surrender—literally, sacrifice—of human life to the survival interest, grandeur, and vanity of the principality.

Yet, again and again, with nations no less than other powers, history discloses that the actual meaning of such human idolatry of nations, institutions, or other principalities is death. Death is the only moral significance which a principality proffers human beings. That is to say, whatever intrinsic moral power is embodied in a principality—for a great corporation, profit, for example; or, for a nation, hegemony; or, for an ideology, conformity—that is sooner or later superseded by the greater moral power of death. Corporations die. Nations die. Ideologies die. Death survives them all. Death is—apart from God himself—the greatest moral power in this world, outlasting and subduing all other powers no matter how marvelous they may seem to be for a time being. This means, theologically speaking, that the object of allegiance and servitude, the real idol secreted within all idolatries, the power above all principalities and powers—the idol of the idols—is death. To many humans and, as it were, to themselves, the nations and institutions and assorted principalities may seem to be glorious, autonomous, or everlasting powers, but in fact they are themselves vassals or serfs, acolytes or surrogates, apparitions or agents of death. This is explicitly denoted in the Bible, where the principalities are named as demonic powers—as

82   An Ethic
                                    for Christians and Other Aliens
                                    in a Strange Land

powers of death, or as tempters, or as emissaries of Satan
(Rev. 12:9; cf. Gen. 3:1,14–15).

Parenthetically, it must be noticed that this scene of the
Fall, as I depict it here, is much too simplified. The principalities are not quite so coherent (how, for instance, can
ideology and nationalism be distinguished in Mao's China?),
neither are they arrayed in the world in settled rank or
ordained order, nor are these powers noncompetitive as they
confront human beings. The demonic powers are fallen,
which means they do exist chaotically, apparently thriving
in confusion, rivalry, and complexity. Demonic claims
against human life in society are multiple, simultaneous,
and competing, as anybody can realize who has endured
conflicting simultaneous loyalties to family and nation and
work or whatever.

(4) an inverse dominion

Pretending autonomy from God, these creatures are
autonomous from human control. In reality they dominate
human beings. Relying upon the biblical description, I have
come to think of the relationship of the principalities and
persons as if the Fall means that there has been not only a
loss of dominion by human beings over the rest of Creation
but, more precisely than that, an inversion or a reversal of
dominion. So, now, those very realities of Creation—traditions, institutions, nations—over which humans are said in
the Genesis Creation story to receive dominion and the very
creatures which are called thus into the service and enhancement of human life in society exercise, in the era of
the Fall, dominion over human beings (Gen. 1:26). The
work of the demonic powers in the Fall is the undoing of
Creation (Gen. 6:11–13). The gravest effort of the principalities is the capture of humans in their service, which is
to say, in idolatry of death, whatever external appearance
or particular form that may assume.

Dehumanization is one term of current jargon for the
reversal of dominion between persons and principalities.

Traits of the Principalities

Specific illustrations of it from contemporary American experience abound—in the precedence, for example, of bureaucratic routine over human need in the administration of welfare or of Medicaid; in the brutalization of inmates where imprisonment is really a means of banishing men from human status, hiding them, treating them as animals or as if they were dead as human beings; in the separation of citizens in apartheid, enforced, as the case may be, by urban housing and development schemes, by racial limitations of access to credit, or by the militia; in the social priorities determined by the momentum of technological proliferation, regardless of either environmental or human interests thereby neglected, damaged, or lost; in genocide practiced for generations against Indian Americans; in the customs of male chauvinism; in the fraud and fakery and the perils to human health and safety sponsored by American merchandising methodology.

(5) are some powers benign?

As commonplace and recurrent as such aggressions by the demonic powers against human life in society are and, literally, forever have been and so long as time lasts will be, human beings generally and, it seems, Americans particularly persevere in belaboring the illusion that at least some institutions are benign and viable and within human direction or can be rendered so by discipline or reform or revolution or displacement. The principalities are, it is supposed, capable of being altered so as to respect and serve human life, instead of demeaning and dominating human life, provided there is a sufficient human will to accomplish this.

I suggest this to be, however, a virtually incredible view. It is both too naïve and too narrow, incorrigible, and a stance which is both theologically false and empirically unwarranted. It really asserts that the principalities are only somewhat or sometimes fallen and that the Fall is not an essential condition of disorientation, morally equivalent to

84   An Ethic
                       for Christians and Other Aliens
                              in a Strange Land

the estate of death, affecting the whole of Creation in time.
It construes the Fall as a wayward proclivity or corrupti-
bility in institutions and nations and other principalities.
It is, moreover, a remarkable expression of human vanity,
insisting that human dominion over the rest of Creation, if
occasionally ineffectual, is nonetheless retained if humans
have the stamina to exercise it. Empirically, meanwhile,
this position dismisses the enormity and interminability of
human suffering of all sorts prevalent in this world which is
only properly attributable to the fallenness of the principalities and powers. War or famine or pestilence; persecution or repression or slavery—the realities which constitute
the daily fortune of the overwhelming masses of human
beings on the face of the earth and which symbolize, by
embracing all experience which is apparently less grotesque,
the threat of death for every human being—issue from the
parasitical posture of the principalities toward human life.
Corporations and nations and other demonic powers re-
strict, control, and consume human life in order to sustain
and extend and prosper their own survival.

The biblical comprehension is realistic about this, exposing the wantonness of Babylon, the great nation who
destroys, squanders, devours human life for the sake of her
own vainglory and enrichment and power (Rev. 18:7-8, 24).

(6) principalities as aggressors

The delusion which captivates so many humans and specifically so many Americans, that the principalities are
somehow exempted from the Fall and vouchsafed from
death and thus are viable or can be so rendered, is directly
relative to the victims of the demonic powers. Human
beings do not readily recognize their victim status in relation to the principalities. To illustrate concretely: the
American legal system, a principality, has seemed to me—a
white, middle-class, Harvard-educated lawyer—to be civil
and fair; to be viable, both theoretically and, *so far as I have
been concerned,* practically. Only recently, and only once, so

Traits of the Principalities

far, have I had occasion to see myself as a victim rather than as an apparent beneficiary of that system. That one event in which I felt I was being assaulted and violated as a person by this system, being victimized by the principality, being threatened with death, was in the utterance of charges, without support in fact or law, against me in connection with my friendship and hospitality for Daniel Berrigan. Even in those circumstances, I could muster an apologetic for the legal system. That is, I could conclude that the attempted prosecution was a political matter, an aberrant use of the law, a form of harassment, and take comfort that the charges were found insufficient and improper by the court and dismissed. So, even in the Block Island case, it is difficult for me to regard myself, in relation to the legal system, vis-à-vis *that* principality as a victim.

My inability or reluctance to visualize myself as suffering the aggressions of the principality against human life is not, however, definitive as to this characteristic of all principalities. How must this same American legal system have seemed to George Jackson, who died under such ambiguous circumstances in San Quentin after a dozen years confinement issuing from conviction of a theft of $70? Another aberration? One wishes that might be true, but the facts are persuasively contrary. American blacks have consistently, for all the generations in which there have been American blacks, been dealt with by the legal system in the same way that this principality disposed of George Jackson. How viable was the Bill of Rights at the time of its ratification to a black chattel slave? Aberration? There is no other honest way to describe the relation between the law in America and American blacks, between this principality and these human beings, than in terms of the aggressions of the legal system against human life. For blacks in the U.S.A. (to cite no other nonwhites of which the same must be said) the law, in a quite overwhelming sense, in the legislatures, in the courts, in law enforcement and administration is now, as it always has been, an enemy: a harasser, an invader, an oppressor. And this is the law's reality not

86

**An Ethic
for Christians and Other Aliens
in a Strange Land**

only in notorious circumstances, like chattel slavery or the era of the lynch mobs or the generations of voter intimidation and disenfranchisement or in the assassinations of black leaders or in the vindictiveness of welfare policy or in the official persecution of black politics or in the ingenious and tireless evasions of school desegregation (contrived as much in the White House as in any school board) or in the sometimes fatal abuse of black prisoners, but also, and perhaps more significantly, in the apparently petty, routine, daily assaults and importunities which blacks suffer under the guise of legality. Any talk of injustice for blacks as merely occasional or aberrant is, simply, racist sophistry.

On the other hand, if the law's aggressions against blacks are admitted and, for the sake of maintaining the illusion that institutions are or can be made truly viable, it is suggested that the law in America remains nonetheless viable for white citizens or that there are in fact racially identifiable two legal systems, then the most crucial issue respecting the supposed viability of principalities emerges. If the American legal system seems viable for me and other white Americans but is not so for citizens who are black, or for any others, then *how,* as the dual commandment would ask, in the *name of humanity, can it be affirmed as viable for me or for any human being?*

(7) victims of the principalities

All this is, manifestly, a matter affecting all nations and societies, all principalities and powers, all human beings. It is the same issue, for example, discerned by a few persons, including some Christians, during the Nazi regime's extermination of Jews, when those persons apprehended that all human beings had become victims of the Nazi principality and that the Jews who were the immediate and literal victims were so as the representatives of all humanity.

This same surrogate status of the victim of demonic power is mentioned with great emphasis in the Babylon story in

Traits of the Principalities

Revelation where the doom of the great nation is described as a vindication for the persecutions and murders of all saints and prophets (Rev. 16:6, 19:2, 20:4). Saints and prophets, let it be said, are not particularly to be thought of as heroes or as otherwise romantic figures. They are not superpeople: a saint is just an exemplary human being, a mature and free person, a humanized human being; a prophet is one whose work is intercession for human life, the faithful public advocacy of human life in society, the proclamation and provocation of redemption. The concern in Revelation for the victims of demonic aggressions illuminates how specific victims (like the Jews under Nazism or the blacks under the American legal system) are neither forlorn nor abandoned because of the radically ecumenical character of their representation of all human beings in all of time.

Though I had had no anticipation of it, this same issue of the significance of the victim of the demonic was one which I was repeatedly required to confront in my Harlem law practice. Nothing has happened to contest the practical conclusion, which is at the same time the theological truth, I reached in that experience, namely, that the inherited system of so-called justice in this nation is profoundly and generically racist. That situation is quite as threatening to whites as to blacks, albeit the threat to whites may seem less obvious and less conspicuous and is less recognized. For white citizens to be blinded to this is a victimization of them as human beings—consigning them to a delusive state where conscience is dead—just as much as the more blatant and public dehumanization visited upon blacks.

(8) acolytes of the demonic powers

If there be knowing victims of the principalities, if there indeed be saints and prophets, there are many victims who do not realize it, and there are persons who are eager slaves to these idols. Often these acolytes of the demonic seem oblivious to how the principalities tyrannize and corrupt

88

**An Ethic
for Christians and Other Aliens
in a Strange Land**

their humanness. In Revelation, the kings and merchants and traders seem startled and bewildered at Babylon's doom (Rev. 18:9–17). There are those who actually define their humanity as nonhuman or subhuman loyalty and diligence to the interests and appetites of the principalities. There are many who are dumb and complacent in their captivity by institutions, traditions, and similar powers. There are persons who have become automatons. There are humans who know of no alternative to an existence in vassalage to the principalities. There are people who are programed and propagandized, conditioned and conformed, intimidated and manipulated, fabricated and consigned to role-playing. There are human beings who are demonically possessed.

There are spectacular or extreme examples of dehumanized obeisance to the demonic—such as the Emperor Domitian or, perhaps, King George III or Hitler or Stalin. But what may be of greater significance in the present American situation are more ordinary persons whose humanity is jeopardized or humiliated by the routines of technocracy—like assembly-line workers or salespeople or consumers or promoters or bureaucrats or suburbanites. The servility to ideological, racial, class, or institutional powers of victims such as these is so numerous and commonplace in mass society that it is seldom challenged, or, for that matter, much noticed.

Beyond those who are rendered virtual robots are those called leaders.

The unrelenting, manifold, versatile, ingenious aggressions of the principalities against human life in society, the victimization of human beings—sometimes brutally, sometimes subtly; sometimes meeting resistance, sometimes with ready assent—by the demonic powers exposes a crucial aspect of the contemporary American social crisis. The American problem is not so simple that it can be attributed to a few—or even many—evil men in high places, any more than it can be blamed on long-haired youth or on a handful of black revolutionaries. Besides, our men in high places are not exceptionally immoral; they are, on the contrary, quite ordi-

Traits of the Principalities

narily moral. In truth, the conspicuous moral fact about our generals, our industrialists, our scientists, our commercial and political leaders is that they are the most obvious and pathetic prisoners in American society. There is unleashed among the principalities in this society a ruthless, self-proliferating, all-consuming institutional process which assaults, dispirits, defeats, and destroys human life even among, and *primarily* among, those persons in positions of institutional leadership. They are left with titles but without effectual authority; with the trappings of power, but without control over the institutions they head; in nominal command, but bereft of dominion. These same principalities, as has been mentioned, threaten and defy and enslave human beings of other status in diverse ways, but the most poignant victim of the demonic in America today is the so-called leader.

It is not surprising, thus, to find—in addition to the ranks of those whose conformity to and idolatry of the principalities means that they are automatons or puppets—some persons, reputed leaders attended by the trappings of high office, who are enthralled by their own enslavement and consider themselves rewarded for it, and who conceive of their own dehumanization as justification or moral superiority.

(9) rivalry among the powers

The scene of turmoil and confusion associated with the demonic powers becomes acute when it is recognized that these are rival, competitive powers despite the fact that, at times, they seem to confront human life as compatible or collaborating powers. All alliances among the principalities (the reciprocal arrangements of the Pentagon, some self-styled think tanks, and the weapons industries furnish an example) are transient and expedient. Such liaisons are aptly described in Revelation by terms like "fornication," "sorcery," or "playing the wanton" (Rev. 18:7–15, 23).

From a human point of view, the principalities may in specific circumstances appear to be conspiring or collaborating together against human beings and human life (among

90   **An Ethic**
for Christians and Other Aliens
in a Strange Land

corporations, price-fixing agreements or product control
pacts furnish instances). Yet the basic conflict among all
principalities remains, though it be subdued or concealed
for awhile, because the only morality governing each principality is its own survival as over against every other principality, as well as over against human beings and, indeed,
the rest of Creation. That this singular fixation—a purpose to
survive—is futile does not diminish the fierceness of the
competition and strife among principalities. It has no efficacy
against death; sooner or later, in one way or another, it is
empirically defeated by death so that when a nation or an
institution strives so mightily to survive it is engaged in
absurd tribute to death.

Men are veritably besieged, on all sides, at every moment
simultaneously by these claims and strivings of the various
powers, each seeking to dominate, usurp, or take a person's
time, attention, abilities, effort; each grasping at life itself;
each demanding idolatrous service and loyalty. In such
tumult it becomes very difficult for a human being even to
identify the idols which would possess him.

Commercial athletics in America, for an example, represent a prominent and aggressive principality and—one might
suppose—a more or less innocuous one. Yet the operation of
this demonic power has significant *political* importance. By
diverting citizens from politics and by preoccupying their
concern with sports instead of politics, by distraction and
also by substitution, it provides a vicarious involvement
in place of politics. American commercial sports have a
political significance in this nation markedly similar to that
of circuses and athletic spectacles in Imperial Rome. It is a
short transition from such popularized arena events, diversions, and entertainments to the staging of persecutions,
punishments, and executions as public spectacles. The
Chicago trial, the Harrisburg indictments, and many of the
cases involving Black Panthers are notable examples of how
political repression can be transposed into the equivalent of
a sporting event for the morbid entertainment of citizens
thus diverted from concern for their own rights, their own

Traits of the Principalities

freedom, their own lives, not to mention those of the conspicuously persecuted. The political inattention and default occasioned by preoccupation with conventional commercial sports is just one way in which people are morally softened to the point where they become ready to be spectators at official persecutions and to applaud the lions when they devour their prey.

There are less dramatic ways in which the principalities expediently relate to one another. An American illustration is in how the white middle classes are kept in political conformity—in demonic captivity—in idolatry—by manipulation of the economy through inflation, the engineering of employment and unemployment, and the management of credit. One recalls, in this connection, that in the aftermath of the student outcries against the infanticide committed at Kent State, the federal authorities exerted themselves strenuously to cut scholarship funds, drastically curtail student loans, and practically render students unemployable during the summer months immediately following the student protests. While it is unlikely to have been the only contributing factor—there was relatedly also a great fatigue and much despair—these economic reprisals had substantial success in quashing the expression of dissidence on the campuses. Very many students heard the message that they would be denied aid or credit or needed jobs to complete their education unless they reverted to quietism, unless they conformed politically.

It is a stratagem of the political principalities familiar to the parents of most students. They, along with the rest of the majority classes, are often so assailed with the immediate problems of managing their mortgages and other debts, so much at the mercy of a fragile, inflated credit system, so desperate to retain employment in their status, that their energies and capabilities as human beings are depleted in coping with these demands alone. Whatever the state of their conscience or whatever their intentions, they are left with little or no capacity to become informed or involved in the issues of politics and society. Thus, the manipulation of these

92   **An Ethic
for Christians and Other Aliens
in a Strange Land**

economic factors becomes a means of effectual political control, and citizens who are too distracted or exhausted to
become involved are consigned to ignorance and conformity
and, as has been put, to being the silent majority. This is yet
another form of dehumanization, another way in which the
powers of death victimize human life, turning humans into
automatons.

(10) a morality of survival

The principalities and powers in this or any other society
engage in their assaults against human beings and in their
undoing of human life in society with extraordinary ploy
and guile, deception and charade, babel and falsity. (See
Matt. 12:45; Luke 8:2.) The Babylon episode in Revelation
pictures a scene of final incongruity and distortion. The
principalities thrive in chaos, as has been said. Confusion
attends all the works and stratagems of these powers; after
all, death is confusion in its ultimate connotation.

More than any other recent American happening, the
Vietnam war has documented and dramatized this very condition among this nation's leaders and managers. The war
has exposed the process by which a principality or conglomeration of principalities beguiles and entraps men in courses
of action which wantonly debilitate and destroy human life.
The Pentagon Papers are remarkable and instructive in set-
ting forth this manipulation, this conjuring, this insatiable
appetite for human sacrifice typical of ideological and institutional powers. The public version of these claims of the
demonic powers against human beings commonly sounds
laudable and offers human beings grandiose promises for
their safety, prosperity, virtue, even immortality. Thus, during the ordeal in Southeast Asia of the past decade, Americans have been successively induced to squander life on a
scale so prodigious it appalls imagination and defies calcula-
tion for the sake of stopping the alleged threat of Communist
China or of securing "self-determination" for the Vietnamese
or of hindering the so-called domino theory or of vindicating

Traits of the Principalities

American "honor" or of serving the "national security" interests. And though each and all of these are shams and have long since been known as such, the hold of the military-technological-industrial complex upon the American people has remained tenacious.

The principalities have great resilience; the death game which they play continues, adapting its means of dominating human beings to the sole morality which governs all demonic powers so long as they exist—survival. To put it very plainly, concealed within the public rhetoric justifying the Southeast Asian war (and all that the war has meant as napalm, defoliation, body counts, search-and-destroy operations, saturation bombing, and as abandoned domestic needs, persecution of dissenters, political imprisonments, the alienation of the young, the moral dissipation of leaders and common citizens alike) has been the purpose of supporting and serving the Pentagon and the whole array of war principalities which the Pentagon symbolizes. To speak of the Indochinese war in terms of the relation of principalities and human beings is, bluntly, to expose the survival of the Pentagon and its satellite or adjoining principalities as the purpose of the war. This is one reason why, of course, this war has been more a symptom than a cause of the American social crisis. It is why, also, whenever the war can be said to have ended, no essential change will have been wrought in the nation.

So let it be reiterated that the theological conclusion here (the survival of the principalities is the secret purpose of the war) does not classify America's leaders as nitwits or as wicked, though some in fact be either or both, but discerns their victimization by the principalities and powers to which they are privy. Their servility to the survival interest of these powers depletes them as human beings. They become captivated, dominated, possessed by the demonic. And let it be allowed that this same theological statement is made, and this particular example given, in order to focus upon the extraordinary magnetism and guile of the enslaving or dehumanizing capabilities of the principalities, though,

94   **An Ethic**
                                for Christians and Other Aliens
                                       in a Strange Land

analytically, this does not exhaust the matter. These relationships between the principalities and human beings, in which human life is sacrificed to sustain the demonic, and in which reputed leaders as well as ordinary folk become victims, are more intricate, more complicated, more ambiguous, more tense, more hectic than words can describe. The milieu of the powers and principalities *is* chaos.

And I saw a beast rising out of the sea, with ten horns and seven heads, with ten diadems upon its horns and a blasphemous name upon its heads. And the beast that I saw was like a leopard, its feet were like a bear's, and its mouth was like a lion's mouth. And to it the dragon gave his power and his throne and great authority. One of its heads seemed to have a mortal wound, but its mortal wound was healed, and the whole earth followed the beast with wonder. Men worshiped the dragon, for he had given his authority to the beast, and they worshiped the beast, saying, "Who is like the beast, and who can fight against it?"

And the beast was given a mouth uttering haughty and blasphemous words, and it was allowed to exercise authority for forty-two months; it opened its mouth to utter blasphemies against God, blaspheming his name and his dwelling, that is, those who dwell in heaven. Also it was allowed to make war on the saints and to conquer them. And authority was given it over every tribe and people and tongue and nation, and all who dwell on earth will worship it, every one whose name has not been written before the foundation of the world in the book of life of the Lamb that was slain. If any one has an ear let him hear:

If any one is to be taken captive,
    to captivity he goes;
If any one slays with the sword,
    with the sword must he be slain.

Here is a call for the endurance and faith of the saints.

Revelation 13:1–10

chapter four

Stratagems of the Demonic Powers

If the powers and principalities be legion, so are the means by which they assault, captivate, enslave, and dominate human beings.

Yet all of the demonic claims against human life—for all their number and variegation and in spite of their dynamic qualities and even though they sponsor chaos—have a common denominator. Typically, each and every stratagem and resort of the principalities seeks the death of the specific faculties of rational and moral comprehension which specially distinguish human beings from all other creatures. Whatever form or appearance it may take, demonic aggression always aims at the immobilization or surrender or destruction of the mind and at the neutralization or abandonment or demoralization of the conscience. In the Fall, the purpose and effort of every principality is the dehumanization of human life, *categorically*.

Demonic Tactics and the Prevalence of Babel

I do not attempt, here, any exhaustive account of the ploys and stratagems of the powers that be. But I do cite some of

98   **An Ethic**
for Christians and Other Aliens
in a Strange Land

those most familiar, as a matter of illustration and, moreover, in order to underscore the significance of the verbal
element in the tactics which the principalities mount against
human beings. That the verbal factor is so prominent among
multifarious stratagems is related directly to the fact that
it is the human mind which is being contested and that it is
human conscience which is being threatened by the demonic.
Indeed, I regard the verbal as definitive in all the ploys of
the principalities.

(1) the denial of truth

A rudimentary claim with which the principalities confront and subvert persons is that truth in the sense of eventful and factual matter does not exist. In the place of truth
and appropriating the name of truth are data engineered
and manufactured, programed and propagated by the principality. The truth is usurped and displaced by a self-serving
version of events or facts, with whatever selectivity, distortion, falsehood, manipulation, exaggeration, evasion, con-
coction necessary to maintain the image or enhance the
survival or multiply the coercive capacities of the principality. Instead of truth as that may be disclosed empirically,
the principality furnishes a story fabricated and prefabricated to suit institutional or ideological or similar vested
interests (Rev. 18:23; 20:3, 10).

This ploy is commonplace commercially in American
merchandising and advertising, and has been for a long time.
It has lately been transported into politics and sophisticated
for political purposes on a scale and with a persistence that
is profoundly ominous for human beings. The contention
during the Johnson Presidency about "news management"
documents this view. More recently, in the Nixon administration, official propaganda has been uttered in the context
of a wide-ranging and systematic attack upon the media,
upon newsmen, and upon citizens as auditors of news. In
both of these administrations, the government's propaganda

efforts have been especially concentrated upon selling a prevalent line about the Southeast Asian war. Thus, one is aware that behind both President Johnson and President Nixon have been the machinations of the principality of the Pentagon and the famous industrial-military complex. It is arguable that these two Presidents have been more prisoners and victims of the demonic than sponsors of the reduction of truth to propaganda, or the marketing of official lies, or the intimidation of the media, or the denigration of the First Amendment, or the virtual abolition of credibility in the relationship of government and citizens. Meanwhile, of course, the matter has not been restricted to the Indochina war, but has affected every public issue. If citizens realize, by now, that they have been contemptuously, relentlessly importuned because of untrustworthy versions of Vietnam, they may also begin to sense how their humanity is similarly insulted by official falsehood and propaganda concerning Watergate, the cost of living, taxation, crime, product safety, certain notorious indictments, and practically anything else in which the same political principalities are implicated.

What is most significant in any of these examples is, I think, not the doctoring of the truth per se, but the premise of the principalities that truth is nonexistent, that truth is a fiction, that there can be no thorough or fair or comprehensive or detached discovery and chronicle of events, and that any handling of facts is ideologically or institutionally or otherwise tainted. The recent official aggressions against the media have been based upon this proposition. They take the position that the public media, by definition, have been engaged in indoctrination of a viewpoint and version which, insofar as it departs from the authorized administration line, must be either supplanted by official propaganda or suppressed.

Ominous, indeed! This presumption of the principalities that truth does not exist or cannot with some human diligence be uncovered and conscientiously communicated outreaches the subversion of the discipline of journalism. It abolishes any work of scholarship; it renders education—

100   **An Ethic**
                          for Christians and Other Aliens
                               in a Strange Land

both teaching and learning—partisan and farcical and, in the end, condemns and banishes all uses of human intelligence.

(2) doublespeak and overtalk

The preemption of truth with prefabricated, fictionalized versions of facts and events and the usurpation of truth by propaganda and official lies are stratagems of the demonic powers much facilitated by other language contortions or abuses which the principalities and authorities foster. These include heavy euphemism and coded phrases, the inversion of definitions, jargon, hyperbole, misnomer, slogan, argot, shibboleth, cliché. The powers enthrall, delude, and enslave human beings by estopping comprehension with "doublespeak," as Orwell named it.

Orwell's prototype of the phenomenon of doublespeak declares "war is peace." That very example of doublespeak has become by way of the war in Indochina the literal watchword in America, more than a decade before Orwell's doomsday date of 1984. The plethora of doublespeak contrived and uttered because of this war has been fantastic and evidently inexhaustible. Doublespeak has been solemnly pronounced to deceive citizens, not to mention the Congress, about every escalation, every corruption, every wasted appropriation, every casualty report, every abdication of command responsibility and every insubordination, every atrocity of the war. For example, the cliché "winding down the war" has concealed the most deadly acceleration of firepower and destructive capability in the entire history of warfare on this planet. Again, in 1972, when the United Nations Secretary General verified American bombing of North Vietnamese dams and dikes, potentially jeopardizing as many as five million civilians, the response of the American authorities was classic doublespeak, to wit: "The dikes are not targeted." Or, again, at the outset of the American combat involvement in Vietnam, doublespeak propagated the false conception that the U.S. intervention in Indochina with a handful of heavily subsidized mercenaries was an extension of the grand alliance of World War II.

Demonic Tactics and the Prevalence of Babel

If the war has furnished innumerable specific instances of the doublespeak ploy, so has American racism. In the sixties, it will be recalled, "violence in the streets" became the slogan for suppression of peaceful black protest. More recently, the so-called busing issue refers to barring black migration to white suburbs and to a Presidential pledge of apartheid.

Sometimes doublespeak is overtalk, in which the media themselves so accentuate volume, speed, and redundancy that communication is incapacitated (even where the data transmitted may not be false or deceptive). The auditor's mind is so insulted, inundated, or transfixed by verbal and visual technology that it is crippled or immobilized. Thus Americans had been for so long saturated on newscasts by "Vietnam"—"Vietnam"—"Vietnam"—"war"—"war"—"war" —day after day after day that these words, relayed this way, became signals to the head to turn off.

(3) secrecy and boasts of expertise

An aspect of the delusive aura enveloping the demonic powers is the resort to secrecy. Secrecy in politics is dehumanizing per se; political secrecy begets a ruthless paternalism between regime and citizens which disallows human participation in government and renders human beings hapless against manipulation by trick or propaganda or other babel. (*The Pentagon Papers* document this so far as governmental principalities are concerned; some of the Nader reports on the automobile industry reflect the same issue as to corporate powers.)

Nowadays, Americans are told that secrecy is an indispensable principle of government. Frequently, that claim is embellished by pleas of expertise, that is, the assertion by a principality—like the Pentagon or the CIA or the Kissinger operation—that certain affairs are too sensitive or too complicated for human beings to know about or act upon. In ferocious application this really becomes a boast that bureaucratic routine or computer programming or institutional machinations are superhuman and obviate human abilities

102

**An Ethic
for Christians and Other Aliens
in a Strange Land**

to be informed, to think, to decide and to act, thus relegating the person to a role of spectator or acolyte, submissive and subservient to the requirements of the principality. One common and homely example is known to anyone who has ever tried to register a complaint or otherwise secure his rights in relation to principalities like the telephone company or the power company or a credit card outfit only to find himself in correspondence with a machine, the convenience of which takes priority.

(4) surveillance and harassment

Ancillary to secrecy in politics and commerce and in other realms is surveillance and the abolition of human privacy. The prevalence of industrial and commercial espionage; the monitoring of shoppers and elevator passengers and similar, now commonplace, so-called security precautions affecting ordinary business; the everyday atmosphere of apprehension in which people have come to live in America—all have worked to enlarge greatly the tolerance of citizens toward political surveillance and the loss of privacy. The kind of open society contemplated by the First Amendment seems impossible—and, what is more ominous, seems undesirable— to very many Americans. So there is little outrage when Senate hearings expose illegal military oversight of civilians or when the unprecedented political espionage at the Watergate is exposed or when education (if that is what it can then still be called) is conducted in so many schools in the presence of the police or other "security" forces.

It is not necessary to dwell upon such contemporary citations, however, because surveillance is a very old ploy of the principalities and not at all an innovation of electronics. One recalls that the purpose of the famous journey to Bethlehem of Joseph and the pregnant Mary was to be enrolled for a special tax applicable only to the Jews. It was not only a means by which the Roman occupiers collected revenue but was also a harassment of potential dissidents and a minute political scrutiny of a captive and oppressed people.

(5) exaggeration and deception

In certain situations principalities act or overact so as to engender a belief that their conduct is warranted though no empirical justification exists. It is the audacity of the deceit, the grossness of the falsehood, the sheer excessiveness of the stratagem, the massiveness of the exaggeration which works to gain public credence or acquiescence.

In American merchandising this wantonness has foisted a huge quantity and a startling array of phony, worthless, dangerous goods and services upon purchasers. What may be more significant, such commercial deception has been so common, so widespread, and practiced for such a long time that when the same techniques are politically appropriated human resistance has already been made pliable.

This was a weapon of Nazi anti-Semitism. It was the snare of McCarthyism. This was the devious ploy summoned to defeat Congressman Jerry Voorhes and, later, Helen Gahagan Douglas. Thence the Department of Justice inherited it and has utilized it more often than one cares to recount but, most menacingly so far, to obtain public passivity to the unconstitutional mass arrests in Washington on May Day, 1971.

(6) cursing and conjuring

The demonic powers curse human beings who resist them. I mean the term *curse* quite literally, as a condemnation to death, as a damnation.

In earlier times, American Indians were cursed as savages in order to rationalize genocide. Somewhat similarly, chattel slavery involved cursing blacks as humanly inferior. In more recent American experience, the most effectual instance of cursing, probably, has been the official defamation of the Black Panthers through indictments which conjure images of them as bloodthirsty black revolutionaries. If, by now, most of these prosecutions have failed and the charges have proved to be false or frivolous or fantastic, the curse nonetheless survives.

104   An Ethic
                                 for Christians and Other Aliens
                                      in a Strange Land

From available reports, the principalities and powers of the Soviet Union employ cursing and conjuring more radically and even more recklessly than has yet happened in the United States. Their procedure involves officially diagnosing certain dissenters as insane and then confining and treating them accordingly.

(7) usurpation and absorption

A somewhat more subtle tactic which principalities initiate against humans who do not conform involves the usurpation of human resistance in various ways. No more may be done than a public ritualization of demonstration and official response. But, as has been seen over and over again in what once was the civil rights movement, that can be enough to neutralize a protest. Or far more elaborate schemes may be implemented by the powers that be, as the emerging and expanding role of the government in recent American political trials shows. To be concrete, in the *Catonsville* case in 1968, the federal authorities prosecuted in circumstances where an admitted offense had been committed. If that prosecution can be faulted as overkill in its scope, the government nevertheless kept within the bounds of a prosecution. In the *Harrisburg* trial a few years later, the role of the State reached beyond prosecution of an actual offense; the Department of Justice, there, was implicated by entrapment and use of a paid informer in procuring an alleged or imagined offense. By the time of the *Camden* matter, the political and legal authorities have moved from prosecution to procurement to perpetration, the offense charged having apparently been conceived, sponsored, subsidized, and implemented by agents of the government. Thus the stratagem of the principalities destroys the witness of human resistance by preemption, by fabricating opposition, by a kind of absorption. And, in this manner, the authority of the State to prosecute is transmuted into the power of the State to persecute.

This, too, is no new ploy. In the first century the Apostolic Church suffered enormous pressures to accede to a politically

innocuous position as one of the religious sects of Judaism
existing under a comity of protective custody of the Roman
State. Saint Paul's vocation to preach the gospel of the
resurrection from death to the Gentiles—including even
the Roman authorities—and the traumatic vision which enlightened Saint Peter concerning the same outreach and
mission saved the early Church from being ignominiously
absorbed into the Roman Imperial status quo.

(8) diversion and demoralization

It must be borne in mind that any effort to designate and
describe or illustrate characteristic ploys of the principalities is artificial to the extent that it necessarily abstracts a
particular stratagem from the havoc and frenzy within
which all the powers exist and act. None of these technics
or tactics can be sharply defined; they all overlap, and, moreover, they most commonly can be cited in simultaneous use.
The matter is, of course, further compounded by the intense
relationships among the principalities, by their multiple
rivalries and apparent collaborations as much as by how
many of the powers besiege humans all at once. This is most
pertinent to those ploys which have a distracting or diver-
sionary aspect. That is illustrated by the political importance
in contemporary American society, as has previously been
said, of commercial sports. Sports engage the attention,
time, and energies of multitudes of human beings, diverting them from politics as such and furnishing vicarious
activity in substitution for their participation in political
struggle. More than that, in circumstances where there is
little citizen involvement in the realpolitik of a nation, the
persecution and punishment of nonconforming persons becomes itself a form of public spectacle. For the governing
authorities, and for citizens who acquiesce to a spectator
role, the recent American political prosecutions like those of
Angela Davis or Daniel Ellsberg or Philip Berrigan serve
the same purpose as the arena events involving lions and
Christians in ancient Rome.

This same distracting factor is prominent, obviously,

106

**An Ethic
for Christians and Other Aliens
in a Strange Land**

wherever scapegoats are sacrificed for the survival of principalities, whether the scapegoat be an individual (as
Stokely Carmichael was for awhile in the sixties, for instance) or a class of persons (as welfare recipients have
now become).

There are numberless other diversions convenient to the
demonic powers, some of which may be thought of as divi-
dends which accrue when other ploys are at work. The
relentlessness of multifarious babel in America, for example,
has wrought a fatigue both visceral and intellectual in millions upon millions of Americans. By now truly *de*moralized,
they suffer no conscience and they risk no action. Their
human interest in living is narrowed to meager subsist-
ing; their hope for life is no more than avoiding involvement with other humans and a desire that no one will bother
them. They have lost any expectations for society; they have
no stamina left for confronting the principalities; they are
reduced to docility, lassitude, torpor, profound apathy, and
default. The demoralization of human beings in this fashion
greatly conveniences the totalitarianism of the demonic
powers since the need to resort to persecutions or imprisonments is obviated, as the people are already morally captive.

The Violence of Babel

All of these snares and devices of the principalities represent the reality of babel, and babel is that species of violence
most militant in the present American circumstances.

Babel means the inversion of language, verbal inflation,
libel, rumor, euphemism and coded phrases, rhetorical wantonness, redundancy, hyperbole, such profusion in speech
and sound that comprehension is impaired, nonsense,
sophistry, jargon, noise, incoherence, a chaos of voices and
tongues, falsehood, blasphemy. And, in all of this, babel
means violence.

Babylon is the city of babel. The language and liturgies
of emperor worship in Imperial Rome were babel. The Nazis
practiced babel against the Jews. Babel spawns racism. In
1984, babel is the way advanced technocracy dehumanizes

persons. By the 1970s in America, successive regimes had been so captivated by babel that babel had become the means of ruling the nation, the principal form of coercion employed by the governing authorities against human beings.

It is not just that babel incites violence—though it does, as the American experience in racism for nearly four centuries documents—but, more than that, babel *is* violence. Babel is the violence in which physical and psychical aspects are most intermingled or merged. A straightforward instance has lately been disclosed in Los Angeles. In certain schools contiguous to the Los Angeles International Airport, sound pollution from aircraft movements is so aggravated that teaching and learning are estopped and schoolchildren suffer physical impairment in hearing and, in turn, speech disabilities.

Babel has many, many other violent manifestations than the noise of technology. Essentially, babel targets the faculties of comprehension—sanity and conscience—which distinguish human beings from other creatures. All persons —and all governments, political regimes and similar authorities—have been reminded of that in the remarkable Nobel address of Alexander Solzhenitsyn:

> Let us not forget that violence does not exist by itself and cannot do so; it is necessarily interwoven with lies. Violence finds its only refuge in falsehood, falsehood its only support in violence. Any man who has once acclaimed violence as his method must inexorably choose falsehood as his principle.

Meanwhile, as the tone of Solzhenitsyn's remarks recalls, the relationship of babel and violence is a recurrent biblical theme, notably in Jewish exorcism as practiced during the Captivity, in the episodes in which Jesus confronts demoniacs, in the catechesis of the primitive Church, in the Babylon account in Revelation.

The State as Preeminent Principality

The principalities and powers, despite their several names,

108   An Ethic
                                    for Christians and Other Aliens
                                          in a Strange Land

their multifarious appearances, or their distinguishing characteristics, share a common status as fallen creatures. They
suffer and assert a singular hostility toward human life in
society which expresses their own radical subjugation and
subservience to the power of death.

From a human point of view, it would seem that the
demonic powers are not all equal in life span or capacity for
survival or in prominence or influence. Some appear to be
higher or stronger or more sophisticated or otherwise greater
than others. There is, it appears, a hierarchy of principalities,
in which some of them have precedence over others. This
is evident, beyond the scope of ordinary human observation
and experience, in the way in which history treats the
powers that be. The Roman Empire is thus remembered as
of more importance than ancient Assyria; English colonialism in North America, vestiges of which are still notable,
is interpreted as having more impact than, say, Dutch
colonialism on the same continent. The same tendency is
seen in how the principalities arrange themselves. A hier-
archical order is accorded the principalities within the United
Nations, reflected in the prerogatives of the so-called super-
powers as over against other member nations.

In America, there is a similar appearance of a hierarchy
of principalities: in the pantheon of sports, football is a
larger commercial enterprise than, say, bowling and would
seem to have a wider political influence; incumbency attributes more power, in a variety of ways, to a political party
than is retained by a party out of office; the nation, together
with the governmental institutions, is commonly thought of
as superior to other principalities in society, like the labor
unions or the professions or the universities or the corporations.

I do not know that it can be flatly concluded that there is
an actual hierarchy among the principalities. The scene of
the demonic powers, as human beings behold it, is so chaotic
and so dynamic, so distorted and so hectic, so tense and
tumultuous as to make me pause at saying that certain principalities have a greater inherent dignity than certain others.

The State as Preeminent Principality

Who can say, for instance, which is the greater demonic power, the national administration of the federal government or the Mafia? or the oil industry? or the Central Intelligence Agency? or any of the multinational conglomerates? or the Chase Manhattan Bank?

So I go no further than the statement that there is an *apparent* hierarchy of principalities which fluctuates according to different circumstances, and the status orientation of which is subject to differing constructions or interpretations. It is, at the least, a convenience of thought and language to refer to such a hierarchy. Commonly, the powers are empirically regarded in such a fashion, as has been noticed, and the biblical treatment of the principalities is similar (cf. Rev. 17, 18).

Among all the principalities, in their legion species and diversities, the State has a particular eminence. The State, in this context, names the functional paraphernalia of political authority in a nation, which claims and exercises exclusive practical control of coercive capabilities, or violence, within a nation. The precedence of the State hierarchically among the principalities is related to the jurisdiction asserted by the State over other institutions and powers within a nation. Practically it is symbolized by the police power, taxation, licensing, regulation of corporate organization and activity, the military forces, and the like.

The paramountcy of the State among the demonic powers is probably most readily recognized in tyrannical regimes, ancient or modern. In Revelation, and elsewhere in the Bible where the State is designated as a principality of particular dignity or apparent superiority, the historical realities to which allusions are made are authoritarian or totalitarian (Rev. 13:18). In such a regime any substantive distinctions between the principality of the nation and the principality of the State are lost. The ethos of the nation is absorbed into the apparatus of authority. Or, to put it a bit differently, the spirit and tradition of the nation are abolished by the administration of the State or displaced by a fabricated version of tradition furnished by the State. For all practical pur-

110
An Ethic
for Christians and Other Aliens
in a Strange Land

poses, in a totalitarianism, the nation and the State become merged.

By contrast (though, from a human point of view, it be a very relative matter) in nonauthoritarian societies, the distinguishable but related principalities of the nation and the State remain separated to the extent that the identity and character of the nation are embodied in tradition and inheritance, sometimes expressed constitutionally, or sometimes as common law. This represents and attempts some restraint or discipline upon the exercise of authority and the functioning of the State. In a totalitarianism, what authority does *is* the law, or, alternately, one must say that in such a regime there is no law or constitutional system, or the like, and the law has been displaced by authority or coercive capability. Idealistically, a democratic constitution or a common-law tradition is conceived as representing and protecting human beings against the limited and defined authority of the State. That this may be more recital than practice, more illusory than real, does not alter the fact that law and authority, nation and State name rival principalities whose tensions and conflicts may, inadvertently, if no more than that, benefit human life in society. At the same time, this does not exempt law from subjection to the power of death.

In any case, the State is much regarded historically, analytically, empirically, biblically as the archetypical principality, epitomizing the other principalities and powers and possessing or claiming a certain special status or eminence in the seeming hierarchy of demonic powers. The State, after all, does expose the moral authority of the demonic with a directness and severity that is not so public or so obvious in the existence of most other principalities. That moral authority is death. Every sanction or weapon or policy or procedure—including law where law survives distinct from authority—which the State commands against both human beings and against the other principalities carries the connotation of death, implicitly threatens death, derives from and symbolizes death. Some of the American colonists had a kindred insight when they complained

against the reign of George III to the effect that the power
to tax is the power to destroy. Enumerate the usual prerogatives of the State and it becomes plain that each and every
one of them embodies the meaning of death: exile, imprisonment, slavery, conscription; impeachment, regulation of production or sales or prices or wages or competition or credit;
confiscation, surveillance, execution, war. Whenever the
authority of the State is exercised in such ways as these
the moral basis of that authority remains the same: death.
That is the final sanction of the State and it is the *only* one.

The Antichrist in America

Though, in principle, the same be true of every principality, the very bluntness of death as the State's moral
authority gives rise to the more frequent and familiar association, biblically, of the State with the Antichrist.

Contemporary folk, including churchmen, are, as I observe
them, shy or wary of speaking openly of the Antichrist. The
references in the Book of Revelation, or elsewhere in the
Bible, to the Antichrist are steadfastly ignored. In my own
upbringing and in my adulthood in the Episcopal Church I
can recall not a single instance in which reference to the
Antichrist has been made, apart from one in the *Ministration
of Holy Baptism* in the *Book of Common Prayer*. That reference is too oblique, however, to be very edifying and, inappropriately, would be deleted rather than elucidated, if
proposed revisions in the Prayer Book are adopted.

Among Americans, especially church folk, there is probably a greater need to demythologize the Antichrist than to
demythologize Christ. Of the two names, the former has
been the more neglected, though the latter has been more
abused. When attentive at all to the Antichrist, Americans
have been ready to refer to other places and other times, to
other nations, ideologies, religions, and personages as embodying the Antichrist. Seldom is any such association mentioned in American context.

I suppose the figure of the Antichrist summons medieval

112   An Ethic
                           for Christians and Other Aliens
                                in a Strange Land

connotations or otherwise provokes spooky attributions, superstitions, or the like. One can be spared all that by re-calling the biblical Antichrist which, bluntly, designates the power of death incarnate institutionally or in some other principality or, sometimes, in a person associated with and possessed by demonic power (i.e., Rev. 19:17–20). In the New Testament, the Antichrist is beheld in the emperor or, again, in the throne or the office of the emperor, or, again, in the empire as such, or, again, in the State and its agencies of violence, like the army. Generally, the Antichrist literature in the Bible represents a stylized way of bespeaking the idolatry of death in a nation. This literature has a tone of urgency and compulsion because of the extraordinary extent of self-conscious idolatry in the Roman empire during the first century. The purpose of death always implicit there eventually became very notorious and vulgar and literalistic, resulting in a fusion of nation and State after the manner alluded to above. In some regimes, furthermore, it became personified in the emperor, in whose name the sovereignty of God was claimed. In such a process, which has been known often in the experience of other societies, all other princi-palities are threatened or usurped, absorbed or destroyed, or relegated to vassalage and subservience. The State is deified, and, often, the deity is materialized in the image of the ruler or in the person named as ruler, or in the office of the ruler, though, as has been intimated, in such a meta-morphosis the humanity of that person is annihilated.

This extraordinary phenomenon of demonic possession oc-casions, in the allusions to rulers contemporaneous with the Book of Revelation, the identification of the Emperor Domi-tian as the Antichrist—or, in more recent circumstances, the nomination of Hitler or of Stalin as the Antichrist. Yet be-hind such personifications in emperor or dictator is the exposure of the State as the Antichrist. It is worth remem-bering here that in ancient Jewish tradition there exists an anticipation of the Antichrist explicitly associated with op-pressive rule, exampled by the tale in the Genesis Apo-cryphon of Abraham exorcising the pharaoh.

The Antichrist in America

Where person, ruler, office, and State are merged or united as one demonic power, and where authority and law become synonymous, and where there is an extraordinary apotheosis of the demonic, the Bible warns of the apocalypse impending (Rev. 18:7–8). In Revelation the domination of the power of death politically is so degenerate, wanton, brutal, violent, and antihuman that the narrator speaks in horrific bestial imagery (Rev. 13). The demonic *polis,* the State as Antichrist, is seen as the agent of Satan (Rev. 12:7–17).

Amen. I find the Revelation images apropos in contemporary America, as well as for first century Imperial Rome. They are apt for Babylon, the city in which death reigns. If others find Revelation too vivid or too quaint to suit their view of the present reality in America, the issue raised is one of discernment. As to that, I say this nation, America, like all its predecessors as nations and all other principalities, is ruled by the power of death, and that this truth is as discernible here and now as it was in Ancient Rome. In short, in the Fall, the Apocalypse is always imminent.

The Antichrist, remember, means antihuman as much as the name means anti-God. The Antichrist is the incarnation of death in a nation, institution, or office, or other principality, and/or an image or person associated therewith. And where there is worship of the Antichrist, where there is idolatry of death as embodied in the State, or otherwise, the manifest blasphemy against God and the denigration of worship and the degradation of human life are all aspects of the same happening. A human being cannot be an idolator of the Antichrist without negating his or her humanity, which, at the same time, means without indulgence in a travesty of worship, which, in turn, means without arousing the jealousy of God (cf. Rev. 18:7–8).

In consequence, a biblical person is always wary of claims which the State makes for allegiance, obedience, and service under the rubric called patriotism. Such demands are often put in noble or benign or innocuous terms. But, in any country, the rhetoric and rituals of conformity and obedience to a regime or ruler latently concern idolatry of the Antichrist,

114

**An Ethic
for Christians and Other Aliens
in a Strange Land**

even though that name is not. generally invoked except where the explicit and blatant deification of the State occurs.

Where that happens, the magnitude of the malevolence of the Antichrist for both God and human beings, specifically those who refuse to renounce their humanity and become idolators of death, is exposed. Where that takes place, the State or principality as Antichrist is also revealed as a grotesque parody of Jesus Christ and of his Church in the vocation of the holy nation. Where that comes to pass, the State as Antichrist persecutes or subverts, supersedes and seeks to displace the Church of Christ, even as the Antichrist tries to tempt Christ or entrap Christ or condemn Christ or mock Christ or crucify Christ or overthrow the Lordship of Christ or insinuate that the Antichrist is Christ. In such days, which in some sense are always these days, the churchly institutions are banished or destroyed or converted into functionaries of the State. Those human beings and communities of humans who persevere in fidelity to God and to the gift of their humanity, those who resist death and thus live in Jesus Christ—whether that be a public formality or not—do so under the condemnation of the State in one way or another, be it in ridicule and ostracism, in poverty or imprisonment, as sojourners or fugitives, in clandestine existence, as a confessing movement, or, otherwise, in resistance.

In such circumstances the tension symbolized between Babylon and Jerusalem is gravely exacerbated. What is actually happening is that Babylon assumes the full pretense that she is Jerusalem, which she seeks to validate by assaulting and suppressing the Church living as the Jerusalem emissary. What is transpiring is that the nation—Rome or Nazi Germany or America—lusts to be the holy nation, the Church. And, thus, the Church living in her Jerusalem vocation is an alien in a hostile land.

The American vanity as a nation has, since the origins of America, been Babylonian—boasting, through Presidents, often through pharisees within the churches, through folk religion, and in other ways, that America is Jerusalem. This is neither an innocuous nor benign claim; it is the essence of the doctrine of the Antichrist.

Then I saw thrones, and seated on them were
those to whom judgment was committed. Also I
saw the souls of those who had been beheaded for their
testimony to Jesus and for the word of God, and who
had not worshiped the beast or its image and had not
received its mark on their foreheads or their hands.
They came to life, and reigned with Christ
a thousand years.

Revelation 20:4

chapter five

The Christian in Resistance to Death

Shortly following the end of the Second World War and the ostensible defeat of the Nazi totalitarianism, I spent some time in Europe, in the nations that had suffered occupation. Though still a student, I visited postwar Europe as a participant in several of the early ecumenical conferences, under the aegis, generally, of the World Council of Churches and of the World's Student Christian Federation. Within that ecumenical milieu I was privileged to become acquainted with many of those who had been involved deeply during the occupation and the war in the Resistance to Nazism. Most of these contacts, made so soon after the war, matured into friendships renewed many times as ecumenical affairs would occasion either my own journeys to Europe or American visits of these fellow Christians and colleagues who had resisted Nazism and survived. Philippe Maury was among these, as were Madeline Barot, Bishop Bergrav of Norway, Hans Lilje of Germany, and, later on, Jacques Ellul.

Lately, as might be expected, while totalitarian tendencies have achieved so much momentum and become more obvious

118   An Ethic
                          for Christians and Other Aliens
                                in a Strange Land

and more ominous in America, I have found myself recalling most vividly the conversations I attended with these Resistance leaders in which I listened to them recount their anti-Nazi experiences. It is, I think, the currency of fatigue and moral confusion, of despondency and dissipated morale among citizens of all sorts in the present American circumstances which so quickens these recollections. Whatever the case, two matters from those firsthand exposures to the realities of the Resistance against Nazism have particular pertinence to the contemporary malaise of Americans because of their relevance to the practical situation prevailing in the nation.

Living Humanly in the Midst of Death

One is that the Resistance, undertaken and sustained through the long years of the Nazi ascendancy in which most of Western Europe was conquered and occupied, consisted, day after day, of small efforts. Each one of these, if regarded in itself, seems far too weak, too temporary, too symbolic, too haphazard, too meek, too trivial to be efficacious against the oppressive, monolithic, pervasive presence which Nazism was, both physically and psychically, in the nations which had been defeated and seized. Realistically speaking, those who resisted Nazism did so in an atmosphere in which hope, in its ordinary connotations, had been annihilated. To calculate their actions—abetting escapes, circulating mimeographed news, hiding fugitives, obtaining money or needed documents, engaging in various forms of noncooperation with the occupying authorities or the quisling bureaucrats, wearing armbands, disrupting official communications—in terms of odds against the Nazi efficiency and power and violence and vindictiveness would seem to render their witness ridiculous. The risks for them of persecution, arrest, torture, confinement, death were so disproportionate to any concrete results that could practically be expected that most human beings would have despaired— and, one recalls, most did. Yet these persons persevered in

Living Humanly in the Midst of Death

their audacious, extemporaneous, fragile, puny, foolish Resistance.

Hindsight, of course, has romanticized the Resistance to the Nazi occupations to a glorious episode. The testimonies I heard from some of those who survived are contrary; they were engaged in exceedingly hard and hapless and apparently hopeless tasks.

Why would human beings take such risks? It is not, I think, because they were heroes or because they besought martyrdom; they were, at the outset, like the Apostles, quite ordinary men and women of various and usual stations and occupations in life. How is their tenacity explained? It is not just because of faith. Some were—all that I have known are —Christians, but many of their peers were not. Perhaps more tellingly, most professed Christians, as well as the established churches, did not resist Nazism in ways which truly endangered them. Most significantly, perchance, some only became Christians out of their involvement in the Resistance. Why did these human beings have such uncommon hope?

The answer to such questions is, I believe, that the act of resistance to the power of death incarnate in Nazism was the only means of retaining sanity and conscience. In the circumstances of the Nazi tyranny, *resistance became the only human way to live.*

To exist, under Nazism, in silence, conformity, fear, acquiescence, obeisance, collaboration—to covet "safety" or "security" on the conditions prescribed by the State—caused moral insanity, meant suicide, was fatally dehumanizing, constituted a form of death. Resistance was the only stance worthy of a human being, as much in responsibility to oneself as to all other humans, as the famous Commandment mentions. And if that posture involved grave and constant peril of persecution, imprisonment, or execution, at least one would have lived humanly while taking these risks. Not to resist, on the other hand, involved the certitude of death— of moral death, of the death to one's humanity, of death to sanity and conscience, of the death which possesses humans

120

**An Ethic
for Christians and Other Aliens
in a Strange Land**

profoundly ungrateful for their own lives and for the lives of others.

The other recollection which now visits me from listening to those same Resistance leaders concerns Bible study. While not a practice of the entire Resistance, it strongly engaged the whole confessing movement implicated in that Resistance. Most appropriately, it often included Jewish as well as Christian participants. I recall being slightly bemused at the time of which I am speaking by the strenuous emphasis placed upon Bible study. No doubt that bewilderment reflected my own biblical deprivation, a lack in my American churchly upbringing which I have since struggled gladly to overcome.

In this dimension of the Resistance, the Bible became alive as a means of nurture and communication; *recourse to the Bible was in itself a primary, practical, and essential tactic of resistance.* Bible study furnished the precedent for the free, mature, ecumenical, humanizing style of life which became characteristic of those of the confessing movement. This was an exemplary way—a sacrament, really—which expounded the existential scene of the Resistance. That is, it demonstrated the necessities of acting in transcendence of time within time, of living humanly in the midst of death, of seeing and foreseeing both the apocalyptic and the eschatological in contemporary events. In Bible study within the anti-Nazi Resistance there was an edification of the new, or renewed, life to which human beings are incessantly called by God—or, if you wish it put differently, by the event of their own humanity in this world—and there was, thus, a witness which is veritably incorporated into the original biblical witness.

These same two insights—the integrity of resistance to the power of death as the only way to live humanly and, what is really a particular version of the same truth, the relevance and resilience of the biblical style of life—I have since encountered elsewhere: upon visits to Eastern Europe during the so-called Cold War and the most ruthless phase of the Soviet oppression there; in the Harlem ghetto as the

Living Humanly in the Midst of Death

American black revolt matured; in profound illness; in the actions of such friends and fellow Christians as Daniel and Philip Berrigan.

One wishes, in this connection, to mention affirmatively the American churches. But, alas, that is inhibited because the inherited churches in this society have not been bastions of resistance to demonic power, as embodied in churchly and ecclesiastical forms, in the State, or in other American principalities. Indeed, the churchly denominations and sects have notoriously been among the most benighted institutions in America, remarkably undiscerning so far as the reality of the demonic in history is concerned. And, in the apparent hierarchy of principalities, the American churches have more often than not been among the most menial, manipulated, and degraded vassals of the power of death.

There are multiple reasons for this, some of which have previously been mentioned, notably among them the pagan origins of so many of the churches and sects in this culture. It is no great surprise, then, that so many churches on the contemporary scene are not communities in which the Bible has been esteemed or in which the biblical life-style has been much practiced or in which the Jerusalem vocation is deeply comprehended and loved. Still, if when looking at the churches the marks of Jerusalem are not readily beheld, that does not imply the departure of the Holy Spirit from America or the indifference of God to the militancy of death in the nation or the absence of the biblical witness amidst the American babel and chaos. It means only that human beings must be open to the marks of Jerusalem where they appear—if only, as it were, momentarily—wherever that may be; that one is called to be truly discerning of the Holy Spirit and of all spirits and to be courageous in naming the same. It means further that a Christian freely affirms the biblical life and acknowledges *that* as the Church however, wherever, or whenever that happens and regardless of whether the event of the Church occurs in distance from traditional churchly existence.

Among the conventional ecclesiastical principalities, there

122

**An Ethic
for Christians and Other Aliens
in a Strange Land**

are, mercifully, as have been cited earlier, occasional congregations and paracongregations, and there are laity and clergy and some few ecclesiastics, that stand—together with more ad hoc communities and happenings and people—within the continuity of the biblical witness. Taken together, I believe, these constitute an emergent confessing movement in the United States: spontaneous, episodic, radically ecumenical, irregular in polity, zealous in living, extemporaneous in action, new and renewed, conscientious, meek, poor. It is to these phenomena, far more profound and much more widespread than is commonly recognized, that a person must look to sight the exemplary Church of Jesus Christ acting as harbinger of the holy nation. It is in this confessing movement that the Jerusalem parable is verified, now, in America, right in the midst of the ruin of Babylon's churches and miscellaneous death shrines.

Violence and False Hope

The biblical witness and mode of living as a pilgrim community and as an alien people in this world—the Jerusalem image of the Church evident in various appearances here and there and now and then, as precedented during the first century persecutions, as exampled in the Resistance to the Nazi totalitarianism, or, lately, in a quickening confessing movement in America—evinces distinctive understandings of nationhood and citizenship, of society and social change, of politics and revolution, of social ethics and political tactics, of hope and action.

(1) the impotence of revolution

The word *revolution* summons pictures of barricades in the streets, insurrection and sabotage, guerrilla fighting, and evokes memories of great, classical revolutions: the Soviet Revolution, or the French Revolution, or, most of all, the American Revolution. It should, as well, bring to mind the comparable contemporary revolutions in the Third World.

Violence and False Hope

For biblical people there are many other remembrances: the long and anguished chronicle of Israel's resistance to pharaohs and emperors; the poignant juxtaposition of Jesus condemned and crucified between two political agitators, having been himself substituted there for Barabbas, the convicted insurrectionist; the revolutionary fervor of the zealotic factions of Judaism coinciding with the emergence of the new Church and her struggles and controversies concerning her ecumenical mission and her political role.

In all of these associations and recollections, Christians stand in dialectical posture, recognizing the hopes which human beings attach to revolutionary causes, and affirming that much. Simultaneously Christians realize an inherent inefficacy in classical revolution because of its reliance upon the very same moral authority as the regime or system which it threatens to overthrow and succeed—death—and thus, they resist that.

Revolutionary sanctions of death cannot overcome the social purpose of death in any status quo. In any revolution, the means of death cannot transcend death, much less defeat or destroy death. At the most, it can alter the guise of death or make death appear more attractive. This remains the reality even though a revolution is represented in the loftiest human idealism, or where the provocations to revolt have become humanly intolerable and revolution seems the only recourse, or where the cause is humanly just, informed by worthy intentions and sensible precautions against corruption, abuse, and scandal.

The issue here is the vitality of the moral power of death in the origins of revolution, and not merely one of distortion or abandonment or compromise of initial revolutionary aims, nor one of subsequent counterrevolutionary events undoing a splendid revolutionary charter. To illustrate, in the American Revolution, the revolutionary ethic embodied in the Declaration of Independence and the constitutional system suffered in the inception the radical contradiction of the property ethic—especially as that was epitomized in chattel slavery. That generic conflict between human beings and

124

**An Ethic
for Christians and Other Aliens
in a Strange Land**

property claims evidences the moral presence of death in the beginnings of the nation; that original decadence in the American revolutionary cause is now in climax in the present crisis of the nation; the troubles today in America have not materialized out of nothing but have been implicit throughout the American experience as a nation seized and possessed by the power of death. Thus, in 1776, some white Americans decreed their freedom from the obstinate and arbitrary tyranny of the British throne; two centuries later all Americans have suffered mock-regal administrations in the White House as capricious and ruthless as the rule of George III. And the poignant corollary in American history between George III and the Presidency now is no happenstance but is a conspicuous portent of the essential bondage to death in which the nation has been throughout its history.

This is, let it be reiterated, no peculiar condition of America. It represents only the American version of the fallenness of all nations and of all causes and of all revolutions. Doubtless many citizens in the U.S.A. are encumbered—by idolatry of death—from assessing the American Revolution and the nation as anything but glorious and unique, but perhaps this vanity will not hinder concrete insight into the fallen estate or condition of death of other nations. Recall, for instance, the devastating exposure of the demonic powers in Kierkegaard's critique of church and society in, of all places, Denmark, a century ago. Or, consider the implications in terms of commitment to death as social purpose in such a small, supposedly placid, ostensibly pacifist nation as Switzerland, where the banking and investment facilities are geared to service the enterprises of multinational conglomerates, Asian mandarins, and principalities like the Mafia. Few Americans, I suppose, would have difficulty in viewing the Soviet totalitarianism as antihuman or the Soviet Revolution as demonic event. Ample further illustrations are available: people are beginning to understand now that the Industrial Revolution, whatever it promises, occasions environmental plunder. We know also that technology unleashed from human dominion means, among other things, ubiquitous surveillance and Orwellian intimidation of human beings.

These are all footnotes concerning the reign of death over nations, revolutions, assorted principalities. In the context of Babylon as a parable for America today, the moral outcome of the Second World War furnishes the most cogent and paradoxical illustration. It now becomes clear—twenty-five years or so afterwards—that the practical ending of the Second World War in the surrender to the Allied Powers of Nazi Germany, and then Japan, was morally inconclusive. As a defeat for or destruction of totalitarianism or of the reliance upon war, brutality, deception, fear, or other forms of physical or psychological violence characteristic of totalitarianism, it accomplished little or nothing. Although militarily and territorially, America and the Allies won the war, little more can be claimed. It has lately been evidenced, ruefully, that economically the war was no victory for the United States. It has been increasingly evident since 1945, acutely so within the past decade, that morally the demonic spirit incarnate in the Axis powers won the war. The illusion has been that, in the aftermath of the Second World War, America succeeded British imperialism and French colonialism in the world, but the truth is that America succeeded Nazi Germany. That is to say, the ethos of Nazism, the mentality of Nazism, the social ethic of Nazism survives, prospers, and more and more prevails in specific American versions—not literally identical to the particulars of Nazism, but nonetheless having the same moral identity as Nazism— which can be symbolized and summarized in three words: *war, racism, genocide.* A quarter century after the ostensible defeat of the Nazi totalitarianism, the morality of Nazism thrives in American circumstances which were, at war's end, already hospitable to death and to the idolatry of death in the nation.

What, then, must be said of the Second World War? Was the enormous effort to destroy Nazism some grotesquely futile struggle? If the United States could have remained out of the war, should she have done so? There are no answers

126   An Ethic
                                  for Christians and Other Aliens
                                        in a Strange Land

to such questions, apart from God's judgment alone, which, in time, remains hidden and mysterious. Yet the very magnitude and versatility of the power of death incarnate in Nazi Germany and the heavy and urgent reliance upon that very same power of death in prosecuting war against Nazism would seem enough to edify human beings that death is the only possible victor in *any* war, that from a human point of view there are no glorious wars—no wars which humanize, no wars of salvation, no just wars—and, at the least, cause human beings to beware of the transmutations of the power of death certain to appear in the aftermath of any war.

Is the anti-Nazi Resistance, particularly that faction of it which issued from the confessing movement of Christians, morally invalidated by the extraordinary resilience of demonic power?

I am bold enough to think not. The anti-Nazi Resistance witness would be vitiated only if those involved in it were naïve enough—and, coincidentally, unbiblical enough—to suppose that the vocation to oppose and transcend the power of death, the calling to live humanly in the midst of death, could be perfected and finished in some immediate involvement like the Resistance to Nazism in the occupied countries, whereas that very vocation is unceasing and incessant. That vocation continues as long as time, itself, persevering throughout every change in situation. If, with the cessation of the Second World War, the anti-Nazi Resistance can be said to have come to an end, the resistance to the power of death did not then cease, nor did the necessity of that resistance then diminish. *That* resistance goes on wherever human beings truly esteem the gift of their own humanity, which at the same time means (whether it is notarized or not) wherever human beings esteem the Word of God.

(2) the ubiquity and versatility of violence

Underneath such questions as these pertaining to the moral presence of death in revolution and war is the long

Violence and False Hope

belabored problem of whether resort to violence can ever be rationalized or condoned by Christians. The historic and hackneyed disputes about that I forbear to regurgitate here, as influential as they may have been or may still be, because they are so biblically specious. In such controversies, nowadays, Christians and professed Christians in America, and elsewhere, overlook or ignore some very elementary aspects of the issue of violence. That is as much the case with political activists and those seeking fundamental social change as with quietists and similar collaborators with incumbent authority, with pacifists as well as with zealots, with pietists of the left and with pietists of the right.

The most astonishing oversight is the most elementary biblical truth concerning violence, namely, violence is normative in the Fall (Gen. 3:4–11).

Violence describes all of the multifarious, inverted, broken, distorted and ruptured relationships characteristic of the present history of this world. Violence is the undoing of Creation. Violence is the moral confusion and practical chaos which, so long as time lasts, disrupts and displaces the truth and peace of Creation, which the Bible denominates as the Fall. Violence is the reign of death in this world and violence is the name of all and any of the works of death.

It is, I suppose, a consequence of the fallenness of human life that human beings so frequently suppose, curiously, that in this world only human beings are fallen. That notion—popularized in America by both adherents of the social gospel and of evangelicalism—is categorically unbiblical. The biblical insight is that the *whole* of Creation is fallen; thus, the violence which is ubiquitous in the Fall afflicts and affects all creatures, not human beings alone. It includes those creatures called the principalities and powers and, among them, preeminently the nations. And, as has been emphasized, the nations and the other powers are fallen, so to speak, autonomously; their fallen status is not derivative from the fallenness of human life.

The ubiquity of violence as the normative estate for all creatures—nations no less than persons—in the Fall should

128   **An Ethic**
                          for Christians and Other Aliens
                              in a Strange Land

recall another elementary feature of violence: its versatility. Violence is often visible, but sometimes violence is invisible; violence may be corporate or it may be personal. There is violence which is visceral and violence which is mechanical; there is violence against property and violence against people; and though each generally, if not invariably, accompanies the other, physical violence and psychological violence are distinguishable.

Violence and Guilt

No violence is private. On the contrary, violence is so dynamic, variegated, and pervasive that all violence must be regarded as essentially political. Even apparently isolated or remote or unilateral violence inherently implicates every human, and every other creature. In the exposition of the old law in the Sermon on the Mount, Jesus pointed to this when he construed anger as murder (Matt. 5:21–22). The violence which Jesus suffered on the Cross becomes the most notorious political event in all history (see John 19:19–22). In the Babylon story in Revelation the most prominent political fact is the violence of Babylon's existence (i.e., Rev. 18:9–24).

The violence of the Fall is *so* political, so penetrating, and so pervasive that even the victims of violence are not innocent and even those who advocate nonviolence are not absolved. No human being is guiltless of any violence. There are never any innocent bystanders. No creature is exempted or exonerated from corporate and collective responsibility in violence.

Americans have known repeatedly in recent times furious, if futile, efforts of humans and institutions to evade or gainsay or otherwise obviate the common guilt for violence in connection with the famous assassinations, and with racial conflict, and with the My Lai massacre, and with the infanticide at Kent State, and with the Attica murders, and with the doomsday bombing of Vietnamese and Cambodians.

For Christians, if for no others, corporate social guilt is

Violence and Guilt

a central biblical theme. It cannot, therefore, be rationalized or put aside. In the Old Testament it is emphasized as a matter of inheritance—the sins of the fathers being visited upon their offspring and heirs—and hence is not something which selection or choice controls. It is a matter of the solidarity of humans in the Fall. In its broadest connotations in the Old Testament, every human being is an heir of Adam and suffers the same alienation from self and from other persons and creatures—which also means estrangement from God—as Adam is described as knowing. If such a conception of inheritance seems stern or somewhat fatalistic to anyone, let it be remembered that in the New Testament reconciliation is a gift to which all men become heirs. In the Fall we are inheritors of Adam but by the grace of God we become heirs of Christ (Rom. 5:12–21).

Inherited guilt actually inversely expresses, thus, the vocation of human beings to love one another. It indicates how, in any particular circumstances, the responsibility of human beings for each other extends to the whole of humanity throughout time. Nowhere is that more cogently signified than in the New Testament drama of Christ's Crucifixion. In that event the secular authorities of Rome and the ecclesiastical hierarchy of Israel are implicated by the accusation, trial, conviction, and condemnation of Christ, not only in their own names and on behalf of their own interests and those of the institutions which they serve, but as spokesmen for all men everywhere and as representatives of all the principalities whatsoever in the whole of history. Moreover, not only Judas, but all the rest of Christ's disciples, by their defections, become accomplices in the Crucifixion and stand alongside the various authorities as surrogates for the rest of humanity.

The Crucifixion is the preeminent example of transcendence of time within time, of the cosmic converging in the momentary, of the integrity of the ethical within the sacramental, of the dialectical *no* and *yes* characteristic of the biblical witness addressed to the world as it is. So Christians esteem the submission of Christ to the Cross as an inter-

130

An Ethic
for Christians and Other Aliens
in a Strange Land

cession for all human beings throughout history. It is as much for those who came before Christ as for those contemporaneous with him in history or those who come after him. On the Cross, as ancient creeds declare, Christ assumes the burden of the sin of the whole world. In just that way, on the Cross, are all men, together with all principalities, guiltily implicated in the Crucifixion of Christ. The extraordinary claim of universal efficacy in Christ's intercession for the world on the Cross is inextricably joined with the reality of pervasive guilt.

Professed Christians sometimes have attempted, and some churches have sometimes taught, equivocation on the issue of cumulative, corporate guilt in the Crucifixion. That attitude renders superstitious the regard for Jesus Christ as having accomplished on the Cross a saving act to which all human beings and all other creatures are beneficiaries. That is why, incidentally, the ecclesiastical handling of the specific question of the participation of the Jews in the Crucifixion has been so misleading and so sordid. It has traditionally focused upon the guilt of specific Jews living at the time of the condemnation of Jesus and, sometimes, upon the alleged social guilt of all Jews for the Crucifixion. But inherited guilt subsumes specific guilt for the Jews on the scene and the Romans, too. It cannot be narrowed to the Jews alone exactly because in biblical context the Jews *always* act as emissaries of all mankind (e.g., Rom. 4:16–18). Even in the most radical apostasy, the election of the Jews as the exemplary people of God, as priest of the nations, as the representatives of humanity before God is not revoked or modified. So to declare that the Jews are guilty in the Crucifixion is simply to confess that all humans share in that guilt.

Biblically, all men and all principalities are guiltily implicated in the violence which pervades all relationships in the Fall. Though this neither dilutes nor exonerates specific commissions, particular acts of some do not release everyone else of their social guilt, either. We may consider Governor Nelson Rockefeller culpable, in a concrete and immediate

Violence and Guilt

sense, for the slaughter of Attica inmates and hostages. But if we do, we must remember that he is, at the same time, joined in that position by all the rest of us. His guilt does not absolve others; corporate guilt does not relieve him.

In the Fall, human beings remain responsible to one another both as perpetrators of violence and as victims of violence. A literal and conspicuous victim of violence is never alone in the immediate circumstances; he is joined there by his own aggressor. In homicide, a person killed is a victim, but the killer is so dehumanized in the action that he is a victim too. There is no such thing as a solitary victim of violence because there is no way to sever a specific victim from the rest of humanity. This has become very plain lately in the course of the political prosecutions in this country—like Harrisburg or Camden—where the rights of the defendants abused by the government are those which belong to all citizens so that the fate of the accused victimizes every citizen.

The common implication of all human beings in all violence—which is a way of expressing the doctrine of the Fall—refutes the intricate sophistry, still much practiced in the name of the Church, concerning "just wars" or any other resort to violent means for assertedly good ends. If, when you hear a President preach that war will bring a generation of peace, it sounds to you like an absurdity—a monstrous exercise in Orwellian doublespeak—it is because it *is* absurd; it is a lie. Death is the only sanction of violence.

The Bonhoeffer Dilemma

Continuing as a contemporary existential issue is the problem of advocacy and/or recourse to violence—that is, a deadly intent and the use of the literal means of death—as it is posed for persons who are Christians and for congregations or similar communities of Christians. This issue has surfaced in American society since the Second World War, notably in racial conflict, in resistance to the military draft, in protest against the war in Southeast Asia, in rebellion

132
An Ethic
for Christians and Other Aliens
in a Strange Land

against the powers that be, in opposition to the repression of dissidence in the nation.

Amid all the evidences and portents of an encroaching American totalitarianism, one does not forget how poignantly this same issue concerning the ethics and tactics of violence was confronted during the Nazi regime by Dietrich Bonhoeffer and others within the confessing movement. That is particularly striking in view of the widespread acquaintance with and enormous impact of Bonhoeffer's thought and action among Americans following his execution by the Nazis for his participation in an attempt to assassinate Adolph Hitler.

Bonhoeffer's witness has helped to expose the simplistics of ideological pacifism as an answer to the question of whether there can ever be Christian involvement in explicit violence. Just as there were among the first century confessing Christians those who identified with the Jewish zealots in the advocacy of violent tactics against the Roman State, so Bonhoeffer's ethics undo the hypothetical imperatives of doctrinaire or pietistic pacifism. We have bluntly to confront the fact that Christians, through twenty centuries, have been implicated in violence, both as advocates and actors, pacifist abstractions notwithstanding. This points to what is deficient in traditional pacifism or in any other attempt to ideologize the gospel, namely, the attempt to ascertain idealistically whether a projected action approximates the will of God. The stereotype pacifist answer to the issue of Christian participation in violence is inherently misleading and in error because an inappropriate and, indeed, impossible question is being asked. It is a query which seeks assurance beforehand of how God will judge a decision or an act. It is a true conundrum which only betrays an unseemly anxiety for justification quite out of step with a biblical life-style that dares in each and every event to trust the grace of God. No decision, no deed, either violent or nonviolent, is capable of being confidently rationalized as a second-guessing of God's will.

Of the specifics of the historicity of God's judgment,

The Bonhoeffer Dilemma

Christians, in common with all other creatures, know nothing. But of the *character* of his judgment—that is, that his mercy and forgiveness are coincident in judgment—much is known. Thus the issue of Christians privy to violence—as in any actions whatever—is a matter of upholding the freedom of God as judge rather than one of a priori knowledge of his judgment.

In other words, where Christians, in the same frailty and tension as any other human beings, become participants in specific violence they do so confessionally, acknowledging throughout the sin of it. I suggest Christians do not, thereby, engage in violence casually or without aforethought or as a first resort rather than last. (Admittedly, multitudes of professing Christians have become soldiers in practically every army without so much as a pause. Moreover, they have done so with the same kind of self-righteousness that, as I have just complained, often afflicts ideological pacifists.)

Christians become implicated in violence without any excuses for the horror of violence, without any extenuations for the gravity of it, without sublimating the infidelity it symbolizes, without construing violence as justice, without illusions that *their* violence is less culpable than that of anyone else, without special pleading, without vainglory, without ridiculing the grace of God.

*Then I saw heaven opened, and behold, a white horse!
He who sat upon it is called Faithful and True, and in
righteousness he judges and makes war. His eyes are like
a flame of fire, and on his head are many diadems; and
he has a name inscribed which no one knows but himself.
He is clad in a robe dipped in blood, and the name by
which he is called is The Word of God. And the armies of
heaven, arrayed in fine linen, white and pure, followed
him on white horses. From his mouth issues a sharp
sword with which to smite the nations, and he will rule
them with a rod of iron; he will tread the wine press of
the fury of the wrath of God the Almighty. On his robe
and on his thigh he has a name inscribed, King of kings and
Lord of lords.*

Revelation 19:11–16

chapter six

The Efficacy of the Word of God as Hope

If, as I have said, the moral reality of death in the Fall is so mighty, so ubiquitous, so relentless a power, what then?

If Babylon be the story of every nation and, right now, is a parable for America; if, indeed, the Antichrist is incipient in the American technocratic State, what can a citizen do?

If Americans are dehumanized by the violence of babel and brutalized in the social chaos wrought by the demonic powers and principalities, how can a person live?

If there are never just wars, if all revolutions harbor death in their origins as much as in their implementations; if violence is pervasive in time and history and if violence begets violence and if none are innocent of violence, what can a human being say?

If God's judgment be hidden from human insight now, so that we have no clue about whether what we decide and do is right or wrong, why bother to risk decision or action at all?

If Jerusalem, the holy nation, is manifest as the reality of the Church of Christ here and there and now and then, in

138   **An Ethic**
for Christians and Other Aliens
in a Strange Land

curious episodes and other occasions, is that any consolation?

And if, when we do dare decisions and take actions, we know them to be ambiguous and inconsistent, extemporaneous and transient, paradoxical and dialectical—always at once saying *no* and saying *yes*—what witness is that?

If in these days we suffer the imminence of the apocalyptic, where are the eschatological signs in which we may rejoice?

Where is hope?

The biblical response—again, an answer which also has empirical authority—is that hope is known only in the midst of coping with death. Any so-called hope is delusory and false without or apart from the confrontation with the power of death, whatever momentary or circumstantial form that may have. It is a person's involvement in that crisis *in itself* —whatever the apparent outcome—which *is* the definitively humanizing experience. Engagement in specific and incessant struggle against death's rule renders us human. Resistance to death *is* the only way to live humanly in the midst of the Fall.

Thus the citizen of Jerusalem is an alien in Babylon. Hope is reliance upon grace in the face of death; the issue is that of receiving life as a gift, not as a reward and not as a punishment; hope is living constantly, patiently, expectantly, resiliently, joyously in the efficacy of the Word of God.

These remarks are not offered as exhortatory rhetoric. The mode of life I am commending has long since been verified and exampled for humans to behold and as admonishment to the powers and principalities—in the biblical witness in the Bible as such and in other events having biblical integrity. Biblical living, therefore, has certain characteristics and definite capacities.

The Gift of Discernment

The gift of discernment is basic to the genius of the biblical life style.

Discerning signs has to do with comprehending the remarkable in common happenings, with perceiving the saga

The Gift of Discernment

of salvation within the era of the Fall. It has to do with the ability to interpret ordinary events in both apocalyptic and eschatological connotations, to see portents of death where others find progress or success but, simultaneously, to behold tokens of the reality of the Resurrection or hope where others are consigned to confusion or despair. Discerning signs does not seek spectacular proofs or await the miraculous, but, rather, it means sensitivity to the Word of God indwelling in all Creation and transfiguring common history, while remaining radically realistic about death's vitality in all that happens.

This gift is elemental to the work of prophetism as that is known and practiced within the confessing community; indeed, it is discernment which saves prophecy as a biblical vocation from either predestinarianism on one hand, or occult prediction on the other. At the same time, discerning signs is directly related to the possibility of celebration in a sacramental sense, to the vitality of the worship of the people and the quality of that worship for coherence and significance as the worship of God rather than hoax or superstition.

Proximate to the discernment of signs is the discernment of spirits. This gift enables the people of God to distinguish and recognize, identify and expose, report and rebuke the power of death incarnate in nations and institutions or other creatures, or possessing persons, while they also affirm the Word of God incarnate in all of life, exemplified preeminently in Jesus Christ. The discernment of spirits refers to the talent to recognize the Word of God in this world in principalities and persons despite the distortion of fallenness or transcending the moral reality of death permeating everything.

This is the gift which exposes and rebukes idolatry. This is the gift which confounds and undoes blasphemy. Similar to the discernment of signs, the discernment of spirits is inherently political while in practice it has specifically to do with pastoral care, with healing, with the nurture of human life and with the fulfillment of all life.

140   An Ethic
                       for Christians and Other Aliens
                            in a Strange Land

The powers of discernment are held by Saint Paul to be those most necessary to the receipt and effectual use of the many other charismatic gifts (1 Cor. 12). Discernment furnishes the context for other tasks and functions of the people of God. It safeguards against covetousness, pride, trick, exploitation, abuse, or dissipation (1 Cor. 13, 14). Moreover, discernment represents the fulfillment of the promise of Jesus Christ to his disciples that they would receive authority *and* capability by the Holy Spirit to address and to serve all humanity (John 15:18–26). Discernment is bestowed upon them, and those gathered with them, in Pentecost, wherein the Church is born and the Jerusalem vocation is renewed. And discernment is thereafter always evident in practice wherever the Church is alive (see Acts 2:14–21).

These are awesome gifts. They have seemed, perchance, all the more so because the powers of discernment are nowadays so seldom invoked, so little practiced, so erratically verified in the demeanor of the conventional American churches. As with other gifts of the Holy Spirit mentioned in the New Testament, discernment of both signs and spirits has somehow become regarded as something rare and unusual—bizarre, even esoteric, occult, or spooky. We admit discernment as an attribute of the primitive Church but readily suppose that it has disappeared or has been so diluted in the succession of centuries since the Apostolic era that it can no longer be expected to be apparent in any but the most exceptional circumstances.

I have a quite different view of the gifts of God to the Church and to the members of the Church. I regard none of the charismatic gifts—least of all discernment—as fantastic or outlandish, but, on the contrary, as commonplace and usual marks of the Church. Pentecost, in other words, typifies the event of the Church, and that not only during the Apostolic period, but thereafter. The manifestation of the multifarious charismatic gifts, including, most particularly, the exercise of the powers of discernment, is definitive of the Church. No assembly, institution, or congregation

The Gift of Discernment

professing to be of the Church of Christ can be regarded seriously in that profession if these powers and works are not evidenced. If today there is hesitancy or inhibition in apprehending the practice of discernment within any of the American churches it is not because the Holy Spirit has begrudged a gift, but, more likely, because there has been too much timidity in practicing discernment. The problem is not want of accessibility to the Holy Spirit, but rather that the gift has been rejected or abandoned. Indeed, as ancient baptismal affirmations declare, discernment is the elementary, common, and ecumenical gift, intrinsic to the authority which every Christian receives, essential to the efficient use of all other charismatic gifts, characteristic of the mature Christian witness in the present day no less than long ago. There are, of course, risks of vanity and temptations of abuse in the discernment of signs and of spirits, as there are with respect to any of the charismatic gifts; but that does not absolve lassitude or excuse indifference or rationalize inaction or condone equivocation. What chiefly hinders discernment in the contemporary churches is not so much arrogance as it is ingratitude. It is not that church people are too proud, but that they are not bold enough; it is not even very pertinent to this issue that American Christians are apostate, since what is more relevant is that they are adolescent in biblical faith.

Discernment of spirits and discernment of signs generally coincide in the same circumstances or appear as particular versions or dimensions or emphases in the same event. Both have to do with the recognition and exposure of the moral presence of death in history and with the confrontation of the power of death with the Word of God. Thus, to follow my own counsel against timidity in practicing discernment, and to supply concrete examples, I must pose the question: what can the biblical mind perceive in a society, in America now, overrun with the violence of babel?

In the midst of babel, speak the truth.

Two major blunders based upon false perceptions or delusions have repeatedly been indulged by Christians,

142   An Ethic
for Christians and Other Aliens
in a Strange Land

as well as other citizens, who have sought to resist official
violence and to refute babel. One is the presumption of
rationality in the nation's leaders. That presumption is often
coupled with the superstition that incumbency in high office,
notably in the White House, somehow enhances the faculties
of sanity and conscience, whereas the evidence is that oc-
cupancy of the Presidency, or similar heights, is a pathetically dehumanizing ordeal, harmful to both sanity and
conscience. This has become acutely obvious in the past
decade during which the idolatry of death as the nation's
moral purpose has been so grotesquely magnified in the
Indochina war.

It is more accurate, more truthful, to perceive the President as a victim and captive of the principalities and
powers. (*The Pentagon Papers* document and detail the
process by which Presidents and other officials are victimized
by demonic powers.) In fact, the captive status of the person
occupying the office has by now reached such proportions
that the Presidency has become a pseudo-monarchy functioning as an elaborate façade for an incipient technocratic
totalitarianism. That sham points to the second tactical
error: imputing malice to the nation's reputed leaders. If
Mr. Nixon or General Westmoreland or John Mitchell, or
any of their predecessors or any of their successors, can be
said to be wicked men, that is of much less moral significance, or political relevance, than the enthrallment of men
such as these with the power of death and their entrapment
and enslavement by the powers and principalities in relation to which they nominally have office. The critical question is not whether these "leaders" bear malice, but whether
they are captivated and possessed by the violence of babel.

And if they are, if that is what can be discerned, what
then? If this nation, and its reputed leaders, be sorely beset
so specifically by the demonic, what befits the Christian
witness?

In the face of death, live humanly. In the middle of chaos,
celebrate the Word. Amidst babel, I repeat, speak the
truth. Confront the noise and verbiage and falsehood of

death with the truth and potency and efficacy of the Word of God. Know the Word, teach the Word, nurture the Word, preach the Word, defend the Word, incarnate the Word, do the Word, live the Word. And more than that, in the Word of God, expose death and all death's works and wiles, rebuke lies, cast out demons, exorcise, cleanse the possessed, raise those who are dead in mind and conscience.

The Particular Charismatic Gifts

Discernment is a common and ecumenical mark of mature biblical living, but that in no sense implies that discernment is vague or indefinite or generalized. On the contrary, in practice, discernment is specific and timely and historic. In its pointed political use in the first century, the Book of Revelation is, perhaps, the most telling illustration of con-textual realism of the discernment of signs and of spirits in the New Testament. In that same respect Revelation is also most reminiscent of Old Testament prophetism and of the Psalms. Discernment furnishes the ethos within which the other gifts of the Holy Spirit distributed among mem-bers of the body of the Church are expended as witness in the world. The particular charismatic gifts, enumerated in First Corinthians as including teaching, healing, administra-tion, prophecy, speaking in tongues, the working of miracles, helping (there is no indication that this exhausts the ac-counting of gifts), are pragmatically associated in each instance with discernment as the basic gift which dispels hocus-pocus, superstition, pride, fraud, or self-indulgence in the uses of these gifts (1 Cor. 12:28–31; cf. Eph. 4:11–13).

It is a blessing that this is so, since distortions of the charismatic gifts and imitations of them are both quite common. Sects within Christendom have repeatedly ap-peared assembled around one or another abuses of this or that gift. That is very prominent as to healing, prophecy, and tongues, but it is by no means restricted to these gifts. At the same time, it must be kept in mind as a caution concerning any charismatic gifts that the external phe-

144   **An Ethic
for Christians and Other Aliens
in a Strange Land**

nomena pertinent to specific gifts can be manifested in sorcery and antiworship as well as in biblical witness and worship. To the undiscerning, babel may imitate glossolalia; there are false prophets and there are true prophets; healing may be occasioned in very many ways—by voodoo or through the incantations of positive thinking or psychosomatically or by medical arts, or, indeed, by the Devil—and healing can be the work of God; while, if it needs to be mentioned, administration can be demonic or it can be a vocation to enhance human life in society. With reference to any of the particular charismatic gifts, the fact that the outer phenomenon is not in itself a sufficient clue to the authenticity of the happening is what renders discernment so rudimentary to the spending of all the gifts. By the same token, we are admonished in the experience of the Apostolic Church that none of the gifts are to be sought or coveted, none are possessed privately, none are idiosyncratic, none connote achievement or superior status, none are sectarian or divisive (1 Cor. 12:11–13). The gifts are authenticated in practice not by coincident phenomena as such. Rather they are verified where the Church is edified by them, where they contribute to unity in Christ, where they emancipate human beings from the fear and thrall of death, where they glorify the gift of life, where they verify the biblical witness.

The Political Character of the Gifts

It spares Christians, and others, the pitfalls of vain, exotic, individualistic, and exclusive views of the charismatic gifts to treat them, as the Bible does, *politically*. To affirm, as Saint Paul does so strenuously, that the gifts are bestowed by God for the increase and edification of the Church, and, thence, for the enhancement and versatility of the Church's servanthood or priesthood on behalf of the world, is to disclose the *political* significance of the gifts and their uses (1 Cor. 14:13–20). Each and every charismatic gift is concerned with the restoration or renewal of human life in society. All have to do with how, concretely, human beings are enabled to cope with the multiple and variegated claims of death. The charismatic gifts furnish the only powers to which humans have access against the aggressions of the principalities. These gifts dispel idolatry and free human beings to celebrate Creation, which is, biblically speaking, integral to the worship of God. The gifts equip persons to live humanly in the midst of the Fall. *The exercise of these gifts constitutes the essential tactics of resistance to the power of death.*

The manifold political significance of the charismatic gifts is relatively obvious with respect, say, to prophecy, where apocalyptic insight and eschatological foresight converge in utterance of action here and now; or to teaching, especially where the biblical style of teaching in parable is maintained. It is likewise not difficult to recognize in administration, where that is comprehended within the Church's vocation as the holy nation or as the priest to the nations, and where, therefore, a bishop is called to be an exemplary ruler or governor juxtaposed to the thrones and authorities of the nations, and, where, moreover, the ecclesiastical bureaucracy, both in its order and its personnel, has a radical vocation in relation to the bureaucracies of the State considered in the same aspects.

Do not, by the way, be too quick to scoff about administration as a charismatic witness in the American churches. While there is a plethora of instances of ecclesiastical institutions which are demonic, caught up in a self-serving morality of survival like other principalities, there are, at the same time, some notable examples of ecclesiastical administration which can be affirmed as charismatic. A diocese with which I am familiar recently disposed of its headquarters property in order to make the proceeds available for the construction of needed urban housing. Some churchly institutions have lately, if belatedly, struggled to become conscientious about their endowments and investments. And, if the ecclesiastical hierarchies have generally been cowardly and quiet, negating their pastoral offices, now and then a bishop does speak out to interrupt the silence and disrupt the mundane conformity of his peers.

The political connotations of some of the other charismatic

146

**An Ethic
for Christians and Other Aliens
in a Strange Land**

gifts—like glossolalia or healing—may seem less apparent. This is partly because of their neglect and partly because, where not cast aside, these are gifts so often subjected to sectarian, pagan, or unbiblical manipulations or to bizarre, private misapprehensions. Yet these gifts cannot be dismissed as intermittent aberration or discarded, not only because of their biblical precedents, but also because of the frequency and intensity of the revival of charismatic phenomena in traditional churches on the contemporary scene. The recurrence of speaking in tongues within the most conventional of the American churches—in the Episcopal Church and the Presbyterian Church, and, increasingly, in Roman Catholic congregations—as well as the impressive growth and vitality of the historic Pentecostal denominations in America (with all due allowance made for fantasy or other corruption) is simply too persistent to ignore. Where the Holy Spirit enables ecstatic utterance, why is this happening in America now?

(1) glossolalia

Of all the charismatic gifts, glossolalia, as a contemporary happening at least, is probably the most vulnerable to superstition, the gathering of cults, and status pretensions. I wish therefore to remind of every caution already mentioned concerning such distortions of the gifts of the Holy Spirit and, most particularly, to reiterate the rudimentary importance of the powers of discernment and their availability to all biblical people. With tongues, as with other specific gifts, it is edifying, also, to be mindful of the mundane counterparts which are familiar and commonplace. Christians will be relieved of occult or magical or vain misunderstandings of the speaking in tongues if they are appreciative of how often ecstatic speech occurs in ordinary human experience outside the Church. I refer, now, not to curious tongues as in voodoo and other religions and dark arts, but to the rapture and the delighted talk manifested in, for example, adolescent love. Or, for another instance, ecstatic utterance and nonsensical praise are very common in the rituals of patriotism and nationalism as in the blatancy of emperor worship in the first century, or in the Nazi cultus, or in the vulgar insinuations of American culture—or, in short, wherever Babylon is an apt parable.

If free from fantastic views of glossolalia, we are able to focus upon the emphatic political character of this gift. At Pentecost, it will be recalled, the phenomenon of tongues is related concretely to evangelization and to the radically ecumenical scope of the Church in its outreach to all sorts and conditions of human beings, as they are, where they are. At Pentecost, glossolalia manifests the universal efficacy of the Word of God for human life in community (Acts 2: 1–11). At Pentecost, ecstatic utterance means the emancipation of human beings from the bonds of nation, culture, race, language, ethnicity. At Pentecost, speaking in tongues is the sublime and notorious worship of God. According to the account in Acts, there were those who misconstrued that extraordinary public and political happening, supposing the people who praised God rather than the Antichrist to be incoherent and drunk and foolish. If there are those today who view the phenomenon of tongues in a similar way, then such folk are in the same position as those who, hearing from Christ the parables of the Kingdom, were deaf, or who, knowing that Christ healed, took offense at him (Acts 2:13; Matt. 13:13–23; Luke 14:1–6).

I suppose that in the present American circumstances, including the existing condition of the churches here, there are many reasons why the Holy Spirit prompts glossolalia. Surely one is response to the yearning of professed church people for integrity in liturgy and public worship, a need frustrated for so long by divisiveness and sham, vaingloriousness and dissipation, facetiousness and religiosity, joylessness and blasphemy. But if ecstatic worship now disrupts and confounds the travesty of much that has been regularly said and done in churchly sanctuaries, it also exposes the scandal of emperors deemed divine, of principalities treated idolatrously, of national vanity displacing God, of death

148

**An Ethic
for Christians and Other Aliens
in a Strange Land**

extolled, as that has been happening in the wider arena of civic religion in American society. And this, in turn, points to a more profound political meaning of speaking in tongues today in America, which is that the tongues parody the babel. In an American atmosphere heavy-laden with babel, glossolalia bespeaks the rebuke of the Word of God. Ecstatic utterance witnesses the vitality of the Word against the ineptness of blasphemy. Speaking in tongues is a sign of human beings set free by the Word of God from the captivation of official babel and is an encouragement to all persons still oppressed by babel. Within the surveillance of the Antichrist, this spontaneous, unpredictable, unconformable, liberated witness can only be heard as the sound of revolution, though, indeed, it be a much greater portent than that. This speaking in tongues heralds the doom of Babylon, warns of the judgment impending upon the Antichrist, joins in the jubilation of the heavenly chorus when the great city falls.

(2) healing

That all of the charismatic gifts are substantively, if somewhat ironically, political can also be discerned in healing. The central question here is not how healing happens, whether medically or miraculously, or otherwise (though in my own radical illness there has been occasion to write elsewhere, in *A Second Birthday,* about those matters). Healing, seemingly, is a most intimate event, distinct and distant from politics. Yet the healing episodes reported in the New Testament are very much implicated in politics. The healings attributed to Jesus became prominent in provoking his condemnation. In the earliest days of the Church, healings invoking charismatic authority—along with the preaching of the Resurrection—became pretexts for the arrests of some of the Apostles (Acts 3:1–10; 4:1–4). One speculates whether the repeated admonishment of Jesus to maintain silence about his healings has a political meaning; one recollects that Jesus was subjected to political interro-

The Political Character of the Gifts

gation because of reports in circulation about his power to heal (Matt. 9:1–8; Luke 5:17–26). The political implications of healing come to focus most lucently in the remarkable incident of the raising of Lazarus, however, since that was not kept secret (John 11:1–12:19). Far from it, Lazarus accompanied Jesus in the Palm Sunday procession and some scholars conclude that this was what exhausted the temporizing of the political authorities concerning Jesus.

In raising Lazarus, in other words, Jesus reveals what is implicit, but hidden, in all of the healing episodes, that is, his authority over death, his conclusive power over death, his triumph over death and all that death can do and all that death means. To so surpass death is utterly threatening politically; it shakes and shatters the very foundation of political reality because death is, as has been said, the *only* moral and practical sanction of the State. Of course, the political principalities and their vassals would loathe and fear Jesus—and seek to consign him to death—*because he healed,* because he raised Lazarus, because he signified the Resurrection from death, because he exemplified life transcending the moral power of death in this world and this world's strongholds and kingdoms.

(3) exorcism

In this context of the political significance of healing, attention is required to that peculiar form of healing named exorcism. If, in modern Christendom, exorcism as a gift of the Holy Spirit has been generally regarded with apprehension and suppressed, it nevertheless has venerable prominence in the biblical tradition. Not only did Jesus exorcise, but it was part of the Messianic expectation in Old Testament Judaism that the Messiah would have this power. Furthermore, in the primitive Church, exorcism, being one of the gifts specifically promised by Jesus for the mission of the Church, was widely and effectually practiced, according to the New Testament (Acts 10:38; 13:10). Indeed, in the ancient Church, liturgical forms of exorcism were commonly

150

**An Ethic
for Christians and Other Aliens
in a Strange Land**

in use as a preparation for baptism (1 Pet. 5:8; James 4:7). Vestiges of that early practice survive in baptismal rites to the present time, though I find little evidence that these are taken very seriously in instruction for baptism.

Still, exorcism cannot be dismissed as some quaint residue, if only because of its biblical status. Some psalms are liturgical exorcisms. In the Jewish tradition of exorcism, as has been earlier mentioned, there is the story of Abraham exorcising the pharaoh. It seems to me that this citation alone is sufficient to show the contemporary relevance of the gift and the necessity for its practice. And, in fact, exorcism is far more widely implicated in witness today than is usually acknowledged directly, the Lord's Prayer itself being a form of exorcism. Whether many who redundantly and ceremoniously recite the Lord's Prayer are cognizant of it or not, the fact remains that the invocation of the name of God, followed at the end of the prayer by the plea to "deliver us from evil" or from "the evil one," constitutes an act of exorcism (Matt. 6:9–13).

All that has been affirmed about the political connotations of healing must be reaffirmed, of course, about this specific kind of healing. The political significance of exorcism is rendered even more emphatic by the content of the Lord's Prayer and by the political circumstances of the impending condemnation of Christ which attended his commendation of this prayer to his disciples.

Politically informed exorcisms which I believe to be as exemplary as that involving the pharaoh do still occur, if occasionally. This, indeed, was the witness of the Catonsville Nine, when they burned draft records in May of 1968. As those attentive to their trial or those who have read or seen the play about the trial can apprehend, the action at Catonsville was a sacramental protest against the Vietnamese war—a liturgy of exorcism, exactly. It exposed the death idolatry of a nation which napalms children by symbolically submitting the nation to the very power upon which it has relied, by napalming official pieces of paper. It is relevant to understanding the significance of the Catonsville action that the Berrigan brothers and others of the defendants had been involved over a long time, particularly since the extraordinary papacy of John XXIII, in the renewal of the sacramental witness in the liturgical life of Christians. They had become alert to the social and political implications of the mass as a celebration and dramatization of the reconciliation and renewal of Creation or as a portrayal and communication of the Jerusalem reality of the Church of Christ loving and serving the world. The Catonsville action is, thus, a direct outreach of the renewal of the sacramental activity of the sanctuary, a liturgy transposed from altar or kitchen table to a sidewalk outside a Selective Service Board office, a fusion of the sacramental and the ethical standing within the characteristic biblical witness.

Vigilance and Consolation

At the outset of this book, mention was made of the need to comprehend America biblically and of the further need for human beings in this nation to live biblically. These are not grandiose matters, but straightforward issues which point to the unpretentiousness of the Christian task or to the humanizing character of the biblical witness in history.

Thus, the issue of biblical ethics is not expressed in vain efforts to divine the will of God in this or that particular situation. On the contrary, biblical ethics asks how to live humanly in the midst of death's reign. And biblical politics, therefore, as it manifests resistance to the power of death, is, at once, celebration of human life in society. Or, by parable, biblical politics means the practice of the vocation to live as Jerusalem, the holy nation, amidst Babylon.

Biblical living honors the life-style of the people of God set out for us in the Bible. A spontaneous, intimate, and incessant involvement in the biblical Word as such—that is, Bible study—is the most essential nurture of contemporary biblical people while they are involved, patiently and resiliently, in the common affairs of the world. Biblical living means, concretely, practicing the powers of discern-

152   **An Ethic**
for Christians and Other Aliens
in a Strange Land

ment, variously perceiving and exposing the moral presence of death incarnate in the principalities and powers and otherwise. And biblical living means, moreover, utilizing the diverse and particular charismatic gifts as the ethics and tactics of resistance to the power of death in the assurance that these gifts are in their use profoundly, radically, triumphantly humanizing.

Biblical living discloses that the ethical is sacramental, not moralistic or pietistic or religious. The identity of the ethical in the sacramental is, perhaps, most obvious in liturgy, where liturgy retains biblical style and scope and content, where liturgy has eucharistic integrity and is not an absurd theatrical charade disguising the idolatry of death. But the sacramental reality of the ethical is, also, enacted empirically, day by day, transfiguring mundane politics by appealing to the presence of the Word of God in all events.

Biblical living involves, as has been cited, a converted sense of time, a transposed perception of history. The biblical mind beholds history as the epoch of the Fall and recognizes time as a dimension of the death experience. Biblical faith, unlike philosophy or ideology or religion, breaks out of the confinement of linear conceptions of time and confounds sequential doctrines of history. The biblical witness concerns the transcendence of time and the consummation of history, the end of time and the fulfillment of history, freedom from time and the redemption of history. Biblical insight encompasses all things as if in a moment. So, in the same event, in any happening whatever, there is the moral reality of death and there is the incarnation of the Word of God, the demonic and dehumanizing and the power of the Resurrection, the portents of the Apocalypse impending and the signs of the imminence of the Eschaton.

In the timely coincidence of the apocalyptic and the eschatological, biblical people live in vigilance and consolation. Biblical living means watching for and hoping for the next advent of Jesus Christ. Biblical ethics, when all is said and done, concerns his dominion on behalf of human life over time and history or, in other words, the doctrine of Christ as Lord of time and history. Biblical politics has to do with acting now in anticipation of the vindication of Christ as judge of the nations and other principalities, as well as persons. So here and now biblical people live and act, discern and speak, decide and do, in expectancy of Christ's promptness. The excited imagery in Revelation of the Second Coming of the Lord, with midair apparitions and other marvels, may have caused some to dwell upon the texts literalistically—to fix upon the wonders rather than upon the excitement of hope. But we can be saved from so demeaning the Second Coming of Christ if we see that, for all its mystery, the Second Advent is faithful to the mission of the First Advent, and is no disjuncture or disruption. On the contrary, it is the consummation of all that has transpired in Christ's ministry in this world, from the homage of Creation rendered to the Christmas child, through the undoing of death's temptations in the desert, to the secret of every parable and the authority of every healing and exorcism, unto the day alone on the Cross condemned by the principalities and powers, abandoned by everyone, consigned to death, until the Resurrection. Biblical living is watchful for that consummation but does not strive to undo the power of death, knowing that death is already undone and is in no way whatever to be feared and worshiped. Biblical living originates in this consolation.

The politics of death in America—which younger citizens apprehend so strongly in their withdrawal or their cynicism or their despair, and of which American blacks and Indian Americans and other nonwhites have so long and so variously been victimized, and which have consigned the white majority classes to bemusement and consternation, and which has so pathetically dehumanized Presidents and other nominal leaders of the nation—is not a uniquely American problem. According to the Babylon parable this represents a specific historic manifestation of the essential condition of all nations and other principalities. In its historicity, death as social purpose is not only the moral reality of the present

154   An Ethic
                                   for Christians and Other Aliens
                                        in a Strange Land

American regime and society and culture but is the inheritance of the nation. It relates back through all American generations so that the massacre at My Lai or the infanticide at Jackson State or Kent State are comprehended as the implementations of the death ethic evidenced in American origins in genocide against the Indians. The present usurpations of the constitutional system by incumbent authority, jeopardizing the rights and protections of all citizens against the State, are beheld as further instrumentations of an original impairment of the Constitution inherent in the institutionalization of chattel slavery. Among so many things, the plunder of the American environment, in and of itself apocalyptic in its proportions (even if there were no other apocalyptic dimensions to the contemporary American scene), is known to have its sanction in the American death idolatry which bestows precedence upon property over human life. So the fascination with the moral power of death has always been in the nation. It has not just lately materialized. In times of apparent triumph or glory, as in the ostensible victory over the Nazi totalitarianism or when the automobile became commercially feasible or with the advent of technology, as well as in times of obvious crisis and failure, as in the Vietnamese war or in recurrent ecological disasters or in the ghetto riots, it has been present.

These are factual and analytical statements. None of them are volunteered as deprecations, as put-downs, for America. Beyond their factual and analytical justification, they are theological statements. The nation *is* fallen. Americans exist in time, in the era called biblically the Fall. America is a demonic principality, or a complex or constellation or conglomeration of principalities and powers in which death furnishes the meaning, in which death is the reigning idol, enshrined in multifarious forms and guises, enslaving human beings, exacting human sacrifices, capturing and captivating Presidents as well as intimidating and dehumanizing ordinary citizens.

Though history vary, though particular facts be different, the same basic theological statement, by the virtue of the

Vigilance and Consolation

biblical word, can and must be made about every nation.

What then?

Is there no promise for America? Is there no American future different from the present, or from the past? Is there no American dream except nightmare? If America *is* Babylon, and Babylon is *not* Jerusalem—confounding what, all along, so many Americans have been told or taught and have believed—is there any American hope?

The categorical answer is *no.*

The answer informed by the biblical witness is *no.* The answer for those who are Christians is *no,* and, therefore, the answer which Christians commend to other human beings is *no.*

The audacity of human beings who are Americans, in the present national circumstances, to utter that *no* is, paradoxically, the signal of a lively hope, a hope transcending America's bondage to death. It is a hope wrought in realism about this nation: a hope which confronts the fallenness of the American principality; a hope which confesses the nation's death idolatry; a hope emancipated from moral naïveté about any supposed unique destiny for the nation; a hope freed from vainglorious delusions that America is a holy nation.

The courage to say *no* in this sense is in itself a radically humanizing experience. It is a *no* which verifies a waking conscience—not an idiosyncratic exercise but an expression of commonality with the whole of human life and a vocation responsible to all other human beings in the face of the ubiquity and versatility of the power of death at work in the principalities and powers of this world. It is the *no* of conscience which, imitating and preserving the biblical way, Christians sacramentalize in baptism, as the epistle attributed to Saint Peter has reminded all men (1 Pet. 3:4–22).

This *no* is the *no* of resistance to the power of death where, as those who resisted the Nazi totalitarianism have shown, resistance is the only way to live humanly.

From this *no* issues the only hope worthy of human beings, because *no* to death, incarnate in the nation or in any other

156   **An Ethic**
                              for Christians and Other Aliens
                                  in a Strange Land

appearance, means *yes* to the gift of life.

So from death arises new life. Suffering issues in celebration. To be ethical is to live sacramentally. To discern apocalyptic signs heightens the expectation of the eschatological events. In resistance persons live most humanly. *No* to death means *yes* to life.

During the Babylonian captivity, the psalmist cries out: *How shall we sing the Lord's song in a strange land?*

The answer is heard in the jubilation of the heavenly chorus at the doom of Babylon.

*And I saw the holy city, new Jerusalem, coming
down out of heaven from God, prepared as a bride
adorned for her husband; and I heard a great voice
from the throne saying, "Behold, the dwelling of God
is with men. He will dwell with them, and they shall
be his people, and God himself will be with them; he will
wipe away every tear from their eyes, and death shall
be no more, neither shall there be mourning nor
crying nor pain any more, for the former things have
passed away."*

*And he who sat upon the throne said, "Behold, I make
all things new." Also he said, "Write this, for these
words are trustworthy and true." And he said to me, "It
is done! I am the Alpha and the Omega, the beginning
and the end."*

Revelation 21:2–6a